The power of magic flows
through all acts of creation.

The power of magic
harnesses desire.

Make your mark.

Also by T. Thorn Coyle

Non-Fiction

Evolutionary Witchcraft

*Kissing the Limitless: Deep Magic and the Great Work
of Transforming Yourself and the World*

*Make Magic of Your Life:
Passion, Purpose and the Power of Desire*

Crafting a Daily Practice

Fiction

Like Water

Alighting on His Shoulders

Music

Face of a New Day

Give us a Kiss!

Songs for the Waning Year (with Sharon Knight)

Songs for the Strengthening Sun (with Sharon Knight)

Hallowed Light (single)

Invictus (single)

Sigil Magic
For Writers,
Artists, & Other Creatives

T. THORN COYLE

SUNNA

Sigil Magic

Copyright © 2015

T. Thorn Coyle

Solar Cross Publishing/Sunna Press

Cover Art and Design © 2015

Solar Cross Publishing/Sunna Press

Cover Art:

© Pinkbadger | Dreamstime.com – Rune Stone Photo

© Starblue | Dreamstime.com – magic book

Editing:

Dayle Dermatis

ISBN-13: 978-0692493281

(Solar Cross Publishing/Sunna Press)

ISBN-10: 069249328X

Sigil Magic

The World Needs Beauty

The power of magic flows through all acts of creation. The power of magic harnesses desire.

First, we name our desire: to create passionately, to be vital and healthy, to have satisfying work, to manifest and share love. Once desire is named, we set intention. Once we set intention, we train ourselves toward the magic of action, the magic of engaging our will.

This book will help you practice what you need to open your creative flow and activate success—whatever that looks like to you—in all of your creative endeavors. This work can be tailored to any creative venture, including building happy relationships and lives filled with curiosity.

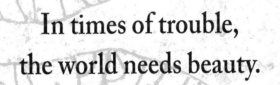

In times of trouble,
the world needs beauty.

Let's create some.

Regarding Sigils

A sigil is a sign, or a seal. I like to think of sigils as "symbolic signatures." What is a signature, but a representation of a being or a thing? A person is not her signature, but her signature represents who she is.

A seal offers a mark of authenticity. What does that mean? The mark is a representation, telling us that the object is backed up with the authority and approval of the owner of the seal.

To design a sigil is to design a representation of one part of yourself that will be your ambassador in the world.

One mark carries your magical intention into the cosmos.

We're going to talk about several ways to design these symbolic signatures. I use several methods myself and will pass along what I've practiced to you. To be clear: I've studied symbol and sigil magic for many years on my own. Magicians and rune masters have passed on some of their methods to me, for which I am grateful. The rest I've figured out through trial and error, the way all creative things must be explored.

Am I a reigning expert on this topic? Not by a long shot. But I've had personal success with these methods and hope you will too.

Though many in-depth books have been written on these topics, I've studied none of them—other than to make a study of my favored symbol systems, mostly the runic alphabet. Everything presented here is simply magic that I have tested and practiced for myself.

There are three main things we will work with in this book: mantras or magical sayings, bind glyphs, and symbols. We will also focus on breath, presence practice, and raising energy.

As an entry point to these discussions, I'm going to ask anyone reading these words to invoke one powerful starting point for both creative endeavors and acts of magic: being aware of the world. Neither magical nor creative success exist in a vacuum, so rooting firmly in our bodies before taking off to other realms becomes both a foundation and anchor for our work.

Let's check in with that right now.

Action

Take a deep breath. Now take another. Notice the breath moving in and out of your nose. What do you smell? What is the room like around you? Are your thoughts racing? Are your emotions engaged? Are they taking over, or stuffed into tension in your shoulders or abdomen? Take another deep breath. Inhale. Exhale. Now let all of those things I just mentioned go.

Slow your breathing down. Try to get your rate of inhalation to match your rate of exhalation. Just. Breathe.

Now, imagine there is a place of stillness at your center, in your body, resting between your navel and your pelvic bowl. Breathe into that center and as you exhale, allow your attention to drop.

Take three long breaths here, and into this place of stillness, drop this question:

What do I want?

Write the answer down. Whether it feels large or small, grandiose or ordinary. Write the answer as fully as you can.

Then take another breath. And into your center, drop a second question:

What do I need?

Write that answer down, too.

Take yet another breath. Re-center yourself. Drop this next question into that still center; like a stone drops into a well, let it sink all the way down:

What do I desire?

Let the sense of this fill your being for awhile. Then write your answer down, as fully as you can, whether it is a word, a sentence, or a page. Allow for the answer to be "I don't know" or for conflicted feelings to be present, if they are. Be as honest with yourself as possible.

Then, center yourself and ask again, this time adding a small detail to the question as you see fit. This is just one example:

What do I desire for my writing,
my creativity, or my career?

Desire is the place where *want* meets *need*. What does your creativity want? What does it need? And what, therefore, do you desire?

Allow yourself to sit with all of these answers. Or better yet, take the answers out for a walk. No matter what the answers were, we'll get back to working with them very soon.

To Begin

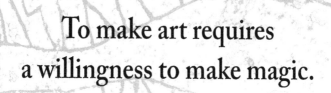

To make art requires
a willingness to make magic.

Are you ready to begin?

Beith: Birch

The first letter of the Ogham alphabet, Birch is propitious for writers, but can be useful for other creatives as well. Birch is fast growing, very fecund and beautiful. It is good to help invoke the energy of beginnings, whether that is the start of a project, or simply the start of this day's session. It is a way to say "I am ready to begin to create." Birch grows easily on bare soil, so is a very good sigil for the empty page or a blank canvas. Some say that it births the rest of the forest. The leaves shimmer beautifully in the sunlight. I've used fallen bark (taking live bark can damage the tree) to write spells on. Birch paper is still made today.

Creation and the Cosmos

Not all acts of creation are magic, but all acts of magic are acts of either creation or destruction. When we join magic with creation, we increase our power and our ability to see our intentions made manifest.

Some people engage in acts of creation and destruction without consciousness. I don't consider these to be acts of magic. For me, magic is the marriage of breath, will, and desire. Without active conscious will, I'm not a magic worker, standing in my center and making my wishes known to all the worlds. I'm just another person, acting willy-nilly, and either suffering or avoiding the consequences, be they good or bad.

Other people say they are working magic, when all they are doing is enacting rituals. These rituals may serve great purposes: rituals can center us, can remind us to pay attention to the sacred, can build community, and can honor Gods, Goddesses, or ancestors. For a ritual to be magic, however, it needs to have both intention and the will to back it up. Magic, no matter how subtle or strong, has power. Power is the energy to do. Therefore, magic also needs a connection to energy in order to operate. This is why so many magicians and witches engage in breath work, or pound on drums, dance in circles, or light bonfires: all of these activities raise energy that the magic worker can tap in order to make the magic work.

What has this to do with writing novels, designing buildings, painting pictures, making films, or composing songs or dances?

To make successful art—art that connects—requires a willingness to make magic. We can all scribble words that will never see the outside of a notebook, or scrawl drawings that we hide in a closet somewhere. Some of that writing or drawing will even be what I'm calling successful art—it will have raised some energy and connected to something, be it our hearts, souls, or the cosmos. Poet Emily Dickinson is a great example of this. She wrote hundreds of poems, baring her mind and her soul. Dickinson paid great attention to the world around her and her inner world. Despite her poems not being published during her lifetime, she connected. Dickinson made magic. That is what gives her poetry lasting impact.

Others of us—scribblers and drawers—never connect. We never take the risk necessary to make magic,
and therefore, to make art. We never muster up the
energy to break through our protections and fight to
illuminate the truth.

Don't think I'm making distinctions between lit-
erature and potboilers here. Don't think I preference
"high art" over "low." Sometimes the potboiler strikes at
greater human mysteries than a carefully constructed literary novel—which is often stripped and polished of the
very magic it set out to create—ever will. Other times,
the literary novel hits deep water and pulls us down in,
swimming into worlds we may have rather avoided, but
need to look at all the same.

Some art creates more magic than others. But all art
needs to connect on some level, even if just to put pleas-
ing shapes or colors next to one another. Think of what
we call "corporate art"—the art that hangs in the lob-
bies of high-rises, or at low-end hotels—it is designed to
be as bland and inoffensive as possible. It is art with no
teeth and little magic because it is art that takes no risks
other than the risk it took to create something at all.

Now, the risk toward any creation at all is a risk I
won't discount, but I want more from us. I want more
from writing, painting, dance, and music. I want more
from architecture. I want more from DJs and MCs. I

grow weary of lack of vision and poor design (yes, any of what I write about in this book can be used for either art or craft, so design falls under its rubric).

Poor design denotes a lack of connection. Bland art does the same.

We are told to "write what you know" not because we need to be faithful only to our lived experiences but *because we need to risk the knowledge that expands us.* When we risk knowledge of ourselves and of the world, a greater magic happens, because we've built a bigger bonfire to dance around.

But we all start where we are. We learn. We light a candle first, and see what illumination that offers. We blow a tentative breath across a dandelion and see which direction the seeds scatter. The stronger the breath, the further the reach of the seeds.

The more deeply we connect with our own hopes, fears, and desires—and the more broadly or pointedly we connect with the cosmos—the stronger our magic and the more potent our art.

We live in times of great upheaval in the midst of the normal every day. People are in pain. People are dying. Land and water are being fractured and poisoned. Greed and inequity run whole countries and ruin many lives. In the midst of all of this, how can we keep ourselves safe anymore? We cannot.

As artists, it is our job to tell the truth. As artists, it is our job to create beauty. As artists, it is our job to offer what ease, joy, or entertainment we can, so that those who are aching can be offered some respite for awhile.

Sometimes our art must challenge others. Sometimes our art needs to offer people a temporary escape. It is not, however, the artist's job to escape. It is the artist's job to confront: to face this world in all of its glorious gorgeousness and weeping despair. Sometimes what art offers is a glimpse of what it means to be brave.

To create art fueled by our magic is to connect with everything we love and fear. If we're going to do this, we should illuminate the tundra with flashes of lightning; we should climb into the deepest caves and scale the tallest hills. We can do all of this by sitting in our homes and plumbing our own souls, but we are better served by also greeting the world each day and night, however, wherever, whenever we can.

We should drink in as much as possible and let it fill us until we pour it out again.

Sometimes in order to create, we need to first destroy. We need to crumble our illusions. We need to blow up the ivory towers that keep us isolated, boring, and safe. Conscious destruction requires our presence and will just as much as conscious creation does. Conscious destruction carries its own magic. It is The Tower of the tarot, struck by divine lightning, or the rune Hagalaz, raining destruction onto crops even as it waters the fields so new seeds can be planted and grow.

In what way are you still not invoking the Power to Dare? What risks are you avoiding taking? Is it being more yourself, more visible on stage or on the page? Is it plumbing some old memories or visioning a something grander and more wild than seems sensible? Is it paring down to the basics, and getting back to your foundations in order to create something truly new from the ground up? We need to assess this over and over, every time our work starts to feel rote or stale, and every time the energy flow feels like it needs to shift.

Will we dare to listen to ourselves? Will we dare to listen to the world, and to our Gods? Will we dare to create from a place of connection instead of from a place that feels well within our comfort zone?

Art breaks and art builds. Whether you are a DJ figuring out what will crack open the dance floor or a writer struggling to be free, I hope the sigil magic in this book will inspire, embolden, and cause something inside you to want to riot. Or maybe the magic held in this book will simply make you want to wake up and create something tomorrow. And the next day. And the day that follows that.

A Story

Gwion Bach stirred Cerridwen's cauldron.

He labored over the giant, bubbling iron pot, sweating and stirring, stirring and sweating. He was doing it because it was his job. The Goddess hired him to stir the brew because she was making an elixir to bestow wisdom on her son, Morfran.

The stories tell us that her son was stupid and ugly. I suspect that those words are just stand-ins for the fact that Morfran likely wasn't a very interesting fellow. And by uninteresting, I mean *not interested.*

In order to become interesting, we must first become interested in the world around us. And most likely, we need to be willing to work as well. People who expect others to do hard labor yet want to reap the rewards of that work themselves, while they sit in comfort and luxury, are neither interesting nor very deserving. No matter how much the world tells us that they are.

The story of Gwion Bach is the story of many things. For our purposes I will say this:

The story of Gwion Bach is the story of showing up to work, and of shifting fantasy and daydreams toward actual desire. Those two ingredients form the rich broth of creativity…and sometimes even lead toward wisdom.

But back to Gwion. Gwion stirred that pot, sometimes drifting into into daydreams on long afternoons. But as he held the mighty wooden paddle in his hands, moving it to and fro in the thickening broth, Gwion also couldn't help but learn. He listened to the sounds of the forest, and watched the animals and birds, observing what he could about their ways. He listened to the rustling of the wind in leaves, and heard the different sounds that oak made compared to yew. He even tried to catch the singing of the stars at night, and the words spoken by the crackling of the fire and hissing coals.

Gwion gathered wood when the pile ran low. He ate quick meals and took quick naps. But mostly, Gwion grew callouses on the palms of his hands from all the stirring that he did.

While Gwion stirred that pot, I'm sure he sometimes fantasized about the life he could be living beyond the drudgery. What else could he do, though? He had to eat. He needed a place to sleep. And besides, he had a contract with a Goddess. He knew the penalty for going back on that.

So Gwion showed up to work, day and night, stirring all the while, for one year and a day.

During that time, I'm sure Morfran also dreamed: he dreamed of what life would be like when the broth was done and he drank of the cauldron of wisdom. Morfran would be smart then! Smarter than smart! Morfran would be wise, and people would consult with him from far and wide, traveling to seek out his insight and his words. Morfran would become someone important. He nestled into a soft bed of leaves on a fine cloak laid out on the forest floor. Morfran waited.

Gwion stirred and dreamed of being master of his own destiny someday. He dreamed of being free of this steaming, face-scorching pot. But still, he stirred. And listened. And watched. And learned.

One day, one long day after the day Gwion began—a full year and the beginnings of one day—Gwion was stirring and stirring, beginning to doze because, though the life in the forest was as vibrant as before, he had grown used to it. He was starting to get bored. He threw some extra wood onto the fire, wishing the broth would hurry up and be done already.

But the stirring continued. The broth was almost done and he couldn't let it burn. Not at this point. Gwion's head began to nod and fall down toward his chest. His stirring slowed. The broth began to boil. Bubbles rose to the surface and one of them burst, sending three searing drops onto his thumb.

Gwion's head snapped up and he shoved the blistering thumb into his mouth.

And with that, Gwion Knew. All the wisdom of all the worlds flooded into him on one expansive wave. Hearing a mighty, groaning, grinding sound, he dropped the great paddle and backed quickly away. The great cauldron cracked, spilling the broth onto the forest floor.

Head pounding with this new-found knowledge, Gwion ran. He ran from the Goddess whom he served, and whose wisdom now coursed through him.

Once she discovered what had happened, Cerridwen gave chase.

On and on they ran, changing shapes: fish and otter, sparrow and hawk, hare and fox, and finally, Gwion transformed himself into a piece of grain, lying amongst other grains. Cerridwen transformed into a black hen and ate him. Gwion remained inside her, being reborn as the Bard Taliesin, the Shining Brow, whose poetry inspired people for generations, and whom many of us know as the Merlin.

Why am I starting off a book on creativity and sigil magic with a story about Gwion Bach? I do it because I've returned to this tale at many junctures during my years of studying magic and making all kinds of art. This story has meaning on so many levels and, of course, can be read from many different angles. I'll share what makes it a significant story for me, personally, and for the work we are embarking on.

Gwion does not wait for inspiration to strike. Gwion shows up to work every day, stirring the cauldron of wisdom. He gathers wood. He stokes the fire. He stirs. He has no idea what the benefit will be, if any, other than it is work he has to do.

Now, we could interpret this as an exploitation of Gwion's labor by Cerridwen, and that's a valid reading. I choose, however, to read this as a metaphor for practice. The Goddess gave him a cauldron to stir and damn it, Gwion stirred that thing. He showed up for a year and a day, stirring all the while. I've been given my own cauldron to stir, and it is my job to show up to that practice every day, too.

Then, when he wasn't expecting it, something changed in the practice and a bubble burst, burning Gwion with the elixir of wisdom. In other words, in the midst of practice, inspiration struck and flooded through him. This happens to me, too. I'll be showing up to spiritual practice every day, and making sure I get in my creative time in the midst of the other work I have to do, and some days I'm very much in the flow. But every day does not start out in that flow, and I don't wait around for it. I've trained myself toward dedication, as though a Goddess had given me the task. And some would say she has. Not Cerridwen in my case, but the particular name matters only to me.

When our heart, soul, or the cosmos has given us a task, showing up to it regularly is a very good idea. The more we show up, the more books, paintings, songs, dances, plays, sculptures, or designs we create. The more art and design we create, from a place of dedication and presence, the better off the whole world is.

Gwion ran with the inspiration. It transformed him and he transformed it, changing shapes and being changed. Finally, he needed a bigger transformation, and was consumed by the very muse/Goddess/taskmaster that gave him the job in the first place. Those of us who've worked on big projects have all felt this at some point, I am sure. The creative endeavor got bigger and stranger than we could even imagine, and we fell into it for awhile, emerging out the other end with even more wisdom than we entered with. A lot more wisdom, more seasoning, more depth, and a greater ability to create what we are meant to.

Taliesin would not have become the great bard whose name rings throughout centuries had he not begun as humble Gwion Bach, stirring a cauldron every day.

We cannot know where our creative journey will take us, but if we commit to it willingly, it will change us for sure. And our changes will influence the world, sometimes in small ways, and sometimes large. What we create might offer a moment of comfort or laughter to someone who needs exactly that. Or it might provide a shift in thinking that alters how someone looks at life. Art does so many things for us all.

Let's stir the cauldron in front of us.

Let's do something for art.

The Well

Deep below the earth and above the ground, the well is a place where two worlds meet. Wells both literally and figuratively give us the water that we need. Without enough water, our cells dry out. There isn't enough oxygen to power our brains. Without enough water, eventually we'll fall asleep. Although dreams are important, in order to create, we need to be awake. When we've been too busy, too distracted, working too hard, doing too much for others, or numbing ourselves, it is time to refill the well. We've run dry. Invoking the well calls inspiration to ourselves by reminding us that, just as the artist inspires others, the artist needs to be inspired. The well also shows us that is the artist's job to bring that which rests deep in the soul up toward the light of day.

The Window

The Hebrew letter Hei. Inspiration means "to draw in breath." This breath is often seen as the drawing in of divinity that resides in the life force flowing all around us. The origin of this letter was a picture of the human with arms upraised, beholding the sacred. The breath taken in that position is the gasp of awe and wonder. Hei also symbolizes a window. This symbol is useful when we've gotten too far from our connection to what we consider sacred. When life has become filled with a series of rote tasks, and not enough wonder, we can open a window to let in some fresh air. We can lift our arms to the sky, our feet planted firmly on this earth, and recall that we are living on a planet, circling the sun. We breathe in life. We exhale connection.

Opening to Inspiration

Inspiration lies everywhere. In every leaf. Each dawn. Every single conversation had, book read, song heard, or scene witnessed. Sometimes what we need is the ability to shift ourselves from ordinary to extraordinary consciousness in order to take these in, and mark that they are, indeed, though ordinary, quite remarkable.

The artist makes everything remarkable. This is part of our job: to remark on things from small to large. To remake the world anew. It is our job to see the beauty in a line of ants carrying food back to the nest, as well as feel the nuisance of them in our kitchen. To feel grateful to the crows picking apart a carcass. To wonder at the effects discordant music has on us. To see how patterns fit together or diverge.

Look at your most ordinary day. What would happen if you were to experience the various components of it with a sense of wonder, rather than taking everything for granted?

To create art is to not take the world for granted.

To create art is to cherish the world, whether in joy or mourning.

In order to create art, we start off with "I wonder" rather than "I know."

Sometimes we need help to do this. We may have grown too accustomed to our surroundings. Our job has ceased to interest us, causing us to shut down and no longer see anything that feels fresh. Relationships may have established their own patterns, so we ignore them and numb ourselves with chocolate, television, social media, or wine.

At these points, we need to interrupt ourselves and our lives. We need to seek out disruption. True disruption, not the facile watchword of business people only seeking to make more money and increase hype. I'm speaking of a rupture from what we think we know and experience to the eye-opening reality that we usually ignore.

As someone who knows many struggling artists, I don't want to suggest that while living in the midst of this capitalist system, we should not make money. If that is currently the simplest unit of exchange, and we don't yet have basic minimum income, so be it. We can work on changing hearts and minds with our art, and do so as ethically as possible. We can use our magic to support that, and increase money, too. And though this is a digression, it is also just another facet of the magic possible in this book: art can re-imagine the structure of society while the artists lives a good life in the middle of it all.

As creatives, what we need is the ability to see through the windows tinted by time, defeat, or lack of attention, and to gaze upon the clear, fresh colors of each day. We need to be able to hear the sounds outside and in, with all their variance, instead of dulled by repetition or drowned in a sea of noise. What helps us to see or hear things more clearly, and with a sense of interest and excitement?

Remember when I asked you to tune in to your body for a moment? This continues the practice, building upon it. What we need to disrupt stultifying patterns is to find new ways to establish a sense of presence. Presence helps us to experience all things anew. Things experienced anew establish a sense of wonder in our souls.

In wonder's wake, we find the seeds of inspiration.

What is the secret of inspiration? It doesn't have to strike like lightning in a California storm—a thing that happens, but is rare enough to require comment. Inspiration can be courted. Inspiration can be cultivated. Inspiration is a garden we can tend, showing up for art and beauty, for pain and discomfort, for the work and effort made each day.

When we tell the cosmos we are ready to be inspired, the cosmos shows up full force and offers us the blooming nasturtium, spicy to taste and orange in color, or the white rose, fragrant with the surprising scent of black licorice warming in the sun.

Inspiration opens itself everywhere, if we are present to its wiles.

People often ask artists—writers in particular—this question: "Where do you get your ideas?"

The answer? Ideas are everywhere. We simply block them out with rote behavior or escapism, with numbing ourselves or with the sheer depths of our fears, or our need to always control the outcome.

When we find ourselves up against a wish to create that feels stronger than a wish to run away, we are open—and present enough—to become inspired.

From inspiration—which for a working artist becomes a daily choice, not a bolt from the blue that we wait for—we create the art that needs to be sent out into the world.

What I'm trying to remind us all of is this: inspiration is both a choice and an opening.

We can prime ourselves for what feels new and fresh by opening all of our senses to the presence of the real. What is real is not pre-packaged. It requires us to be present with it in order to see, to taste, to hear, to feel, to smell, and to experience as though it was the most wondrous thing in the world. It *is* the most wondrous thing in the world. Most people have simply forgotten.

It is the artist's and writer's job to create the pathways that enable people to remember: all of life can be sacred and amazing if we choose to make it so.

We can remember there is magic in this world.

Creativity is a Process

Both creativity and magic are processes. There often isn't a clear beginning or ending point to either. Somewhere in the mix of life, we just decide to call point A "a start" and point Q "an ending." The reality is that creation is happening all the time, and every time we decide to do something and follow through on it, we perform an act of magic.

We also engage in passive acts of magic as well. We undermine ourselves through fear and apathy and call it laziness, or a block, or lack of time. We decide to want complacency and comfort which is an aberration of healthy desire. This sort of passive magic gives us results, and we can see them quite clearly, unfolding in our lives. However, comfortable as those results may seem, they don't usually give us the results actually want. Who wouldn't rather have a sheaf of poems written, or a story, or a song, than to have watched three seasons of television in a two-week binge?

To engage in *active* magic is to begin to create the lives we desire. So it is our job to find the rituals that foster creativity, and to schedule them, and then to use our power to make and to do.

Sometimes magic is an epiphany and an opening. Sometimes creation comes on in one big rush. We can't get the words or images out fast enough. We feel filled with life, with longing, lit with a holy fire inside. Creation pours out. Easy. Vital. Good.

Other times, magic happens like water wears away stone: the slow application of energy over time has an effect.

Sometimes creation is a slow process. It becomes the careful threading of the spider's web, building itself strand by strand, layer upon layer. Creation can take time. And care.

They feel quite different to us, these two states, but I'm here to tell you that there is no difference between the two…if we've made a commitment to the practice of our art. The sense of inspiration ebbs and flows, but the more we've been practicing, the easier it is for the "I feel uninspired today" to shift into "Oh. That worked out just fine. I was able to work." And the whole of our soul and our imagination gets trained to expect that when we show up to work, work happens, no matter what sort of mood we're in.

As I write this, I'm feeling a bit sluggish. My brain isn't snapping and I haven't really found a groove yet today. Why? I didn't get quite enough sleep last night. If I didn't have a word count goal to meet today, it would be easy to just say, "Oh, I've done my other work for the day, and I already wrote four hundred words in another section this morning, isn't that enough?" Instead, I'm back for round two of writing, after some meetings, e-mails, and taking care of other work that needed to be done. I've chosen some music, put in my earbuds, and here I am, communicating with you once again.

Creativity, like love and lust, doesn't look or feel a certain way. I'm being just as creative now as I was yesterday, when the words were flowing out with ease. And yes, I worked my other jobs yesterday, too. It was no more or less a "perfect day" to write than this one.

In both magic and art, we must allow ourselves to have days that feel "on" and days that feel "off" and let them be the same, with no judgment as to quality. Six months from now, we won't recall what we created when, I can guarantee it. Somehow, the work stitches itself together, and what matters in the end is that we got it done.

What matters in the end is keeping a commitment to do our work and make our art. The process doesn't have to feel smooth. The process doesn't need to feel easy. The outcome doesn't even need to please us. What matters is that we write. Or paint. Or dance. Or compose. Or build. Or…

Some days, creativity happens in neat and tidy chunks of time and effort. Schedules or contracts help with this. But even schedules and contracts are imperfect. They are only hopeful maps. We have to walk the territory on our own, however we show up, to the best of our abilities every day. Like me, today. I had hoped to get a lot more written in my morning session, but because of my tired brain, I allowed myself to be distracted, and because I had a client scheduled for 10 a.m., and another meeting after that, I didn't allow myself my other trick of getting out of my home office to go work in a café. I could have, had I just pushed a little, but I chose not to. Instead, I did snatches of work and also managed four hundred words before my client.

And here I am now, later in the afternoon, writing once again.

What I'm trying to say is that creativity can be a messy process. It doesn't have to look neat and pretty and it doesn't even have to go as we had planned. That is perfectly fine. Sometimes we need to dive into some disorder so a new order can emerge. However, there is no need for our creative *intention* to be haphazard. Successful writers have a schedule in which they simply sit down and write. Artists need to draw and paint regularly. The same is true for dancers, musicians, or weavers. Anyone who taps the creative flow knows that it comes more readily if the flow is revisited with regularity.

I'm going to type this again, because it feels important:

We can't wait for inspiration to strike
in order to begin our work.

Inspiration comes during the course of the steady application of pen to paper, or fingertips to keyboard. That is happening for me today. There are things I wasn't even certain that I needed to say, that are getting said. If I hadn't had a muzzy-headed morning, this portion of the book would look very different. And you might have walked away with the mistaken impression that output is always easy for me. It isn't. What is true, however, is that I've put in many years of practicing, and of building up my will, and learning how to better honor my commitments.

We need to be in active relationship with our creative process and we need to commit to that relationship.

What is keeping you from deepening your relationship to your creative process? Is it fear? Anxiety? Depression? Lack of time? Wondering what will happen if you fail? Wondering what will happen if you succeed?

Many of us cycle through all of the above, or more. Others keep getting stuck in one or the other. Breathe into this. Where does the impediment lodge in your body? Stretch the area around it, right now. Then take another breath.

Listen to yourself. Listen to the blockage or resistance. Then breathe again, and listen to your desire.

Some of the most vital creative works come from the very place where resistance and creativity meet. This nexus point generates friction within us, where a "no" bumps up against a "yes." If we can stay with this, and not walk away, we usually find that the energy raised from this friction can by funneled into the task at hand: making art. Telling a story. Moving our bodies across the floor in a way we've never done before.

If you are a person having trouble opening to steady creative flow, the following action item is for you.

Action One

*What is the smallest commitment you can make
to your writing practice or your art?*

Write that down.

Writing down this commitment will help you figure out that all you need to do is take that next step. And then take that step again, and again, according to the perimeters of your commitment. Taking the next step, day after day, tells your psyche that you can indeed do this. Showing up for art and magic also increases your ability to show up with greater commitments, over time.

This "smallest commitment" exercise is also useful for those of us who have overextended ourselves and need to re-group. We can remind ourselves that we don't have to give up entirely, or start over; we just have to offer ourselves a smaller next step as we build up strength again.

Some of us may be in the position where we need to up the ante. Take a bigger risk. Push ourselves a little more, allowing ourselves to stretch our boundaries. If you are a person longing to rise to a bigger challenge, this next action item is for you.

Action Two

What is a commitment that will challenge you to do a little more than you think is currently possible?

(Hint: for me right now, that is writing 1700 words a day, seven days a week. This will need to be renegotiated later, once I'm through the current push with this book.)

Write that down.

Writing down a commitment that feels like a stretch helps us to figure out what needs assistance and what is raring to go. Meeting this commitment offers us a greater understanding of our capacity. Most creatives tend to sell themselves short, or set themselves up to fail, and then give up entirely (we'll talk more about "failing to success" elsewhere). Challenging ourselves by setting a goal just outside our known comfort level teaches us amazing things about ourselves. It shows us that we can often do more than we think we can. It also teaches us the ways in which grandiose plans can be broken down into smaller components and tested, while we accomplish something all the while.

Writing down these commitments will also begin to tell us what our mantra needs to be and which sigils we might make use of. And as I've said, this activity will also help us develop our will.

Neither magic nor art happens without will.

We have to be willing to act, no matter what. Fear or hubris are not good enough excuses to not create what we are meant to, as an offering to this world.

As for my offering, my commitment, I've now written more words than I contracted for today. And in the process of writing, I forgot that I was sluggish, and I entered the flow.

In other words, just showing up for our commitments creates a magic all its own.

The Flow: Awen

This is Welsh and Cornish word that represents creative inspiration. It is linked to the spirit that moves through all things. The root of this word is *breath* and can be seen as similar to mana and prana in other sacred traditions. When we need to access inspiration, the first thing we do is breathe in, carrying oxygen to our brain, and opening back to our connection with the flow of life. Like using the Hebrew letter Hei, calling upon Awen reminds us to breathe in life and to place ourselves back into the sacred flow. For this word, I offer two symbols, the bottom one being a representation of flow that I personally use and the other being a symbol used by many contemporary Druid groups.

The Torch: Kenaz

In the Anglo-Saxon rune poem, Kenaz is described as the torch known by every living man. This is human-made fire used to light the night, illuminate gatherings, and guide the way of those wandering in the dark. We can use Kenaz as a rune for inspiration in several ways. The first is asking for the world to become illuminated to us. A light shining on something tells us to "pay attention," increasing our presence with even the most ordinary of things. The torch is a reminder that we can always choose to light the flame and see. Ideas and inspiration are everywhere; we just need to perceive them. Kenaz helps. Another way we can use Kenaz is when we want our work to be a guide or inspiration to others. We can ask for the help we need to hold the torch aloft.

Summoning Creativity

Someone asked whether it was dangerous to use sigils. Well, my teacher Victor Anderson said, "Anything worthwhile is dangerous," to which I always add, "Not everything dangerous is worthwhile."

Magic is dangerous. Creativity is dangerous. Love is dangerous. Life is dangerous. Of course using sigils will be dangerous. Dangerous how? If we actually put intention and will behind them, we are summoning things with these sigils. We are summoning creative flow, and life force, and success. All of these will change us once they arrive.

Change is dangerous because it upsets the status quo and shakes us out of our comfort zones. But change is inevitable, isn't it? So what shall we choose? Shall we only change via the forces of inertia and by reacting to events outside of ourselves? Or shall we choose to actively invite change into our lives, learning new things and stretching ourselves, sometimes in ways we didn't even know were possible?

Why should we wait for disaster—which sometimes goes by the name of inspiration—to strike? Disaster and inspiration both force change upon us, unwittingly. Sometimes we like it and other times we don't. But either way, we've been waiting around, being acted upon, rather than mustering our will and acting.

By choosing to do magic, we choose to invoke change. I'm for it.

All of that said, I want to *choose* what I'm invoking—or evoking—even while keeping in mind that I won't be controlling the outcome because that is impossible. However, I can set the wheels in motion and point them in the direction I'd like to go.

Classical magic involves the invocation of beings. When doing my sigil work, am I invoking demons or angels? Sometimes. Why do I say that? Sometimes I need to directly encounter my inner demons or angels in order to create the art that is longing to come forth. Do I do classical evocations and summonings and use sigils that are already made for the seventy-two underworld or angelic spirits? No. That's not my magic. I've studied it somewhat, just so I know what it is about, but the only angels and demons I call upon are my own. They are the beings that give power to my writing. I have to be able to face them in order to create something that feels true.

As long as we are avoiding ourselves, we limit our creativity. So yes, perhaps we need a sigil to invoke some of our demons, to give them a new job with all that life energy they've been tying up.

The Demon Perfection, for example, can take on the job to help us do the very best we can while in the flow, rather than stopping us with thoughts of "not good enough" before we even begin. Perhaps the Demon Perfection can help us to perfectly stay on schedule, instead of frittering time away on social media. Perhaps the Demon Perfection can say, "You can't stop until you hit your word count. I don't care how hard the writing feels today." Or "I need you to go out on that stage and take a breath full of confidence because your audience deserves the best performance you can offer today." Those sorts of things are great jobs for our inner demons.

And sometimes we need to invoke our angels: The Angel of Caring. The Angel of Bravery. The Angels of Persistence that keep us showing up.

Both demons and angels can be our allies. We need the power from all of our many human facets. Claiming our power is dangerous. But then, so is not claiming it. Just in a different way. As a writer (and singer, and former semi-professional dancer), I would rather face the danger of claiming art and a creative life than face the danger of living in such a way that constrains my heart and soul.

All right. So sigils, like most things that matter, can be dangerous. But why else might we not want to use certain sigils?

I personally don't use sigils that I'm unfamiliar with. I would want to know something about the culture whose alphabet I'm using, for example. If I'm using the sigil that is associated with a God or Goddess, I want to have a relationship with that being. I'm not a fan of picking random symbols or deities and then expecting them to work for me. That is rude, and not very smart, either. If effective magic and creation require presence and connection, then that needs to include our relationships to the symbols themselves.

Some cultures have rules about their sigils, too. Veves, for example, are traditionally impermanent, usually drawn only for the ceremony at hand. However, a long-term practitioner might make a talisman of them, because they have a strong relationship with the symbol and what it is calling. They aren't using the symbol system in a casual manner.

Do your research before using any symbols that do not come from a culture you currently have a relationship with. Do your best to establish that relationship and to honor the culture and its spirits. Sometimes this also means honoring people who may be currently, actively struggling for their own sovereignty or for justice.

This brings up an important point about magical intention that isn't often mentioned: our intention always exists in context, and so does our magic. Our intention exists in context with the totality of our lives. Any sigil we use also exists in context. If my intention is to have monetary success with my writing and I'm using the sigil of a deity from a currently oppressed people, doesn't it then behoove me to do what I can to help those people? How can I expect monetary success for myself if I don't care about the culture my sigil is coming from?

I've mentioned that I tend to make my own sigils or use old Norse runes. However, if I was drawn to use symbols from Hawaii or from Voudoun practice, for example, I would make certain to be offering money, time, or energy to Hawaiian efforts regarding land rights or doing the same for people of the African diaspora in their struggles for justice. At the end of the book is a link to a podcast on honoring or appropriation. I highly recommend listening to it as you frame your thoughts regarding what symbol systems to use.

In order to do this work well, it is useful to understand the energy currents that flow through all relationships, and then examine whether or not we are in the best relationship we can be with our magic right now.

I'm not saying all of this to paralyze us from movement. We are never going to get any relationship exactly right. However, we can promise ourselves to keep learning, do our best to honor the magic and the symbols, and then let go of our worry in order to get things done.

Take your magic seriously, but not too seriously. Be intent. Be respectful. Then have a light touch with it all and allow yourself to create.

Preparing for Magic and Art

Priming ourselves for the work is done first by observing the habits that undermine our ability to be present in our lives, often causing us to avoid both magic and creativity.

What is the first thing you do in the morning? If your answer is checking e-mail or Facebook, I can almost guarantee that you are undermining your creativity and not opening to magical support as much as you could be.

The first thing I do upon awakening is get out of bed. As soon as my feet touch the floor, I'm at my dresser altar, where I align my soul with breath and say my first prayer of the day. Then I put the kettle on, move to my home office altar, make some offerings to the ancestors, to Freya and Brigid, and then sit in meditation and prayer. Somewhere in this mix I also do various things to get into my body and activate my breath. This changes over time, but I always do something: stretching, breath-work, pushups, squats… Body, breath, spirit, and mind. I engage all of these right away, though the particular form of practice may change over the years.

By the time I am done, the water has boiled and I make myself a cup of tea. Then I'm ready to get to the working part of my day. I still don't check social media or e-mail. I make one quick post to Twitter and Facebook to maintain a connection to those who follow me there. Then I either engage in study and research for writing projects or writing business while drinking my tea, or I get straight to writing, depending on my schedule for the day.

If I allow myself to start following links to stories, or opening emails that of course need answers, my energy begins to fritter itself away.

My practice in the morning is to set my rituals to support the work I most want to do: write. These days I try to get up by 6:30 in order to get enough done before my first spiritual direction clients, which I never sched-ule before 10 a.m. I'm fortunate to have a life where my morning space is expansive. I've also set it up that way.

In my mid-30s, when I was in school full time and working, this meant I was getting out of bed at 5:30 in the morning in order to have enough time on the medi-tation bench and to get some writing in before heading across the city on my long commute to school. I would use my public transit time for reading and study. I got a degree and wrote my first published book this way. I'm not the only one. I know people who arrange their lives toward creativity in the midst of intense, full-time jobs and raising children. Anything is possible. Sometimes we just need to adjust our expectations, get rid of our "all or nothing" attitudes, and find the ways and times we can show up for our art.

The point is, we can turn the simplest things into rituals, and all of our rituals can bolster our ability to choose art and creativity. All of our rituals can bolster our ability to center the things our hearts tell us are important.

Successful creatives all figure this out somehow.

Most writers or artists have little rituals they do to prepare themselves to create. They may not even realize they are doing them, but the activities signal to the unconscious, animal parts of self that "we are getting ready to go there." We are preparing ourselves to enter the creative flow. The dancer puts on the proper clothing and then stretches. The writer waters the plants or makes a cup of coffee. The artist sets out the brushes and paints, or sharpens the pencils. The singer walks around the room, quietly humming, or sipping tea with honey.

So it is with magic. We must prepare.

The most important preparation is to do everything we can to be present. This requires daily cultivation. I'll repeat that over and over throughout this book, just as I do in all my teaching. We can't expect to start from zero every time—whether it be with magic or art—and have success. Sometimes success just happens. It's a fluke. More often though, success happens because we've been preparing for years. Even then, it is still somewhat ruled by chance, but less so.

There came a point in my life where I stopped feeling bewildered by success and lack of success. I stopped talking about luck and replaced that word with "fortune."

My definition of fortune is the place where chance, circumstance, and effort meet. I am fortunate in my life partially because of chance, partially fluke of circumstance, partially because of the efforts of others—for example, though we were poor, my parents found a way to send me to a good school—and partially because of my own efforts.

Though I can remain grateful for the rest, my own effort is the only thing I can really control, so I may as well learn how. I've already mentioned some of the ways that I support my efforts so I don't have to work so hard against the sucking of inertia or distraction.

We all learn through trial and error. To change our luck, though—to step into good fortune—we must start to understand that there are systems of learning and they are not governed solely by chance. Muscles get trained and grow strong through repetition. So does our ability to do magic, to write stories or songs, to paint, or sing, or carve, or engineer, or dance.

Don't leave your good fortune up to chance. Learn by practicing. Increase your odds by showing up on a regular basis.

We'll talk more about this when discussing will development, but the practice of presence and the willingness to commit are important enough to cycle back to multiple times. Throughout the entirety of our lives.

So how do we practice presence?

There are many ways, but my main suggestion is this: to practice presence, keep it simple.

You'll read many elaborate techniques for doing magic, including sigil magic. Some of them are useful. However, if we rely only on elaborate techniques, it becomes easy to find excuses to not show up: because we don't have the time, or the energy. Also, we haven't yet built up our attention. Therefore, I'll offer you a few techniques to help build up presence and attention over time. If you do these every morning, you'll soon find that you can do them several times a day, and from there, you'll develop the ability to do them almost all the time.

It is at that point that you'll notice your personal and creative success increasing. Why? Because you'll always be practicing. You'll cease to have compartmentalized your magic and art from the rest of your life. You will begin living with greater consistency and alignment.

Your life will be more true.

My teacher Cora Anderson used to say, "When your soul is aligned, you can ask the Gods for anything."

So, allow yourself to become aligned. This is both difficult and easy. It can take years, but those years are simply years of practicing. What else do you have to do with your time but practice getting good at your life?

Right now, as I'm typing these words, I feel aware of my butt in the chair, the way my spine, head, and arms are aligned, what my breath is doing, and what is happening with my energy fields. This all comes together to enable me to meet my commitment of writing these words for you to read sometime in my future. It enables us to be here together, now, despite the jump in time.

Without years of practicing commitment and presence, this work would feel exponentially more difficult for me. I would squirm in my chair. I would want to allow myself to be distracted. I would not be present with myself, with you, or with my connection to the flow of inspiration.

Where did I begin? Many years ago, after much struggle, after trying elaborate rituals, after sweating hard with writing, after giving up and trying again, after avoiding the discipline that I thought was too much work, after waiting for the muse, or trying exercises that didn't take me anywhere…I did two things at the suggestion of a teacher.

First, I sat down and learned to *bear* myself. To bear sitting with my complaints, my fears, my grandiosity, my aching back and the foot that kept falling asleep. I learned to be present with myself, and to simply sit with all my parts, allowing them to be part of the greater whole that was on a cushion, breathing.

The second thing I learned was to become aware of my posture. You'd think after years of dance training, I would have had a handle on this. But I didn't. It wasn't until I made a commitment to keep my feet on the floor and to roll my shoulders back, supported by the muscles of my lower back and stomach, that full presence began to slowly emerge.

That's how it worked for me. I pared my practices down to sitting and posture.

Then I added in breath, because both sitting and posture work naturally require it. Conscious breathing is an enormous teacher of pretty much everything. These are always my core practices. All of my other practices emerge from and revolve around being present in my body. My relationships to deity, to art, and my other rituals all begin with my relationship to my body.

Action

We'll talk more about energy work later. That is important too. But the most important thing you can do right now, to help your magical practice and your writing, painting, dancing practice, is this:

Show up to yourself every day. Be with yourself. Sit in outward silence and just notice what comes up. Then adjust your posture and breathe. Slowly. In and out.

Start with the simple things. Begin (or re-commit) today.

To Listen: Ansuz

Odin's rune. This rune is significant for writers in that Odin hung on a tree for nine days, after which he received the runic alphabet. I use this rune to remember that first, I listen to the Gods, the cosmos, or for inspiration, and then I speak or write. I find that if I center myself and listen *first,* the writing flows out with greater ease. If I try to write first, my brain throws up too many blocks, starting with "What if this isn't the correct/best thing to be writing?" Those blocks can continue, of course, spiraling into fear if we let them. It's best to not let fear get that sort of hold on our creative process.

Use this rune to help your inner critic settle down and to open to the divine flow.

To Ignite: the Matchstick

This is a sigil I made up to help light the fires of inspiration. Sometimes we need a little magic to perk us up or get us going. This is like the sigil equivalent of a cup of coffee or tea, with a little extra oomph behind it. If you've been feeling sluggish or unmotivated, this sigil is a good one. It lights a fire in your heart and mind…and under your ass! This sigil isn't for sustained work, but is used only to kick off a project or a session. But that's enough for most of us: all we need is a little push to get started, and then we're good to go. We can design other sigils to help us stay the course.

Starting Where We Are

In a previous section I wrote, "Start with the simple things. Start today."

There will never be a perfect time for us to do our magic. There will never be an ideal time to sit down and write, or to make time to dance, or paint, or compose, or build, or any number of things.

We work with what we have, where we are.

Today, all we can do is show up as centered as we can be. We can prepare for work as much as we can. Today. Tomorrow may not show up at all, but more than likely, tomorrow will arrive and be just as busy—or grief filled, inconveniently scheduled, tired, anxious, distracted, or wanting to party—as today.

We have to stop making excuses to not commit to creativity. We need to reconnect to passion.

A heightened sense of distraction or self-numbing often points to the avoidance or slowing down of our connection to passion. We can't engage with passion if we aren't present in our lives. We can't engage with creativity if we aren't even willing to try.

Regarding starting where we are: we don't have to feel immersed or ignited with passion in order to do our magic or our creative work. But we would do well to notice what our current relationship to passion is and see whether or not we need to open up the flow from a trickle to a stream, or perhaps slow down the torrent that has taken us from passion into obsession.

So let's look at that:

What is our current relationship to passion? How does play, rest, or discipline fit into feeding that? What else feeds passion?

Have we grown obsessed with something, and allowed it to eat our life energy? What practices will bring that tendency further back toward life integration?

Do we feel drained and underwhelmed by life? What practices will revitalize us?

In all cases, we are well served by practicing presence. Going back to sitting. To breath. To posture. Why? First, we must feed presence.

My definition of passion is "full engagement." So our numbing, distracting, or obsessive habits are signs of lack of presence and signs that we are avoiding passion for some reason. This impedes our ability to be with our desire to create, and to show up for creative practice in a steady or meaningful way.

Deep listening is part of presence, and what we find when we listen points to our deeper desires.

First, we notice the pattern. We just observe what the top layer is, such as: "Oh, I'm distracting myself. Okay."

Then, we notice what is beneath the pattern: "Hmm. I wonder if I'm avoiding something here? Is there fear? Or does my desire feel overwhelming? Do I need more rest, but am I not allowing myself to do things that feel rejuvenating because of my to do list?" There are many questions and observations that are likely to come up when we notice beneath the pattern. I've listed only a few.

The thing to do is not to psychologize our patterns, but simply let them be. They will begin to shift over time, through observation and the practice of presence. Meanwhile, keep breathing. Get outside. Go for a walk. Drink a cup of tea. Then ask: "What am I longing for?"

After that, come back to your determination to create. The world needs it. And our magic can help.

Working magic supports the process of building our relationship with creative flow. Powering up a sigil can remind us that our intention is to focus on our writing, on our art. That is the second step toward success.

I've used sigils to help me manifest many things. They help to focus and enliven my intention, and enable me to work in greater alignment with the cosmos.

You can make a yourself a "creativity sigil" or a "focus sigil" to boost your output. You could also make a "1,000 words per day" sigil!

These sorts of sigils are useful to hang above the area where you write—you can draw them on a piece of paper or inscribe them onto metal—or to draw on your computer or notepad. You might also trace them on your forehead before your creative session.

Some people—like author Joanna Penn—find it useful to track writing projects on a paper calendar. She knows what her daily word count goal is and writes her accomplishment on the paper calendar each day, giving herself a bold check mark on days when she hits the goal. This is a great visual reminder to your imagination that progress is happening.

You can use your sigil in this way, too. Every day, write the sigil on the paper calendar in pencil before your creativity session. Then get to work. When you are done with your session, re-trace the sigil in one color if you've made your goal, and in a different color if you fell short of your goal.

We want to retrace the sigil even if we fall short because we still had success! We wrote (or painted for twenty minutes of the hour set aside. Or danced…).

Author Dean Wesley Smith talks about "failing to success," which is an important concept for writers and other creatives. Too often people grow discouraged if they have said "I'm going to write 5,000 words this week" and manage to write 3,000. That 3,000 words is still success. There's no failure when we show up to work.

Working with a focus or creativity sigil helps to keep us on track. Another great thing about using one of these sigils—such as To Fly or To Learn, or To Dawn or To Strike—as a focusing agent is that we get to practice multiple things at once. We get to try out our practices of breath and presence and we get to practice using a sigil to boost our abilities, too. This combination creates a synergy that can build on itself over time, increasing our powers of concentration, creativity, and magic.

Center and Circumference

Though we can begin using sigils for creative focus, I'd like to go over another practice of presence. The more we work on this, the more our magical power increases. We'll get a lot more out of our creative sessions, too.

This practice something I call Center and Circumference, and which many of my clients and students simply call "C&C."

Center and Circumference is a very basic presence exercise as well as a great orientation of self to self and self to place. It reminds us that we have a core and a boundary and that we are part of something larger. Orienting to the world with our own compass, we remember that our lives can have direction, and exist within the maps of up and down, north and south, east and west. Our center becomes the center of the earth, or like the hot heart of the sun that everything else revolves around.

Remaining aware of center offers us a chance to do the writing, make the art, and enact the magic that is clamoring to get out of our minds and hearts and into the world.

It is hard to sit down to write, or work on other creative projects, if we are "beside ourselves" rather than centered from the core on out.

One way people trip themselves up and lose their connection to center is in getting too distracted by what is outside the self, occupying themselves with thoughts of past or future, or with what others will think or say. A second way people forget themselves is forgetting there is an outside world at all, let alone that they are part of that world. They get trapped in navel gazing, or apathy, or sink into despond.

Center and Circumference reminds us to remain part of the whole without losing our sense of self. Both are important to the magic of creativity.

Let's walk through this exercise, which I do every day, multiple times.

Action

Take a breath. I like to touch my tongue very lightly to the front of my soft palate. This allows me to take in greater amounts of air with less effort than breathing with an open mouth or through the nose. Breathing with tongue softly touching the roof of my mouth enables me to start the influx of breath down deep in my belly, allowing the air to move itself up and expand my ribs out as I go. Sometimes I imagine that I can inhale through mouth, nose, and ears all at once. Breathing in this way also makes it easier to regulate my breath, expanding the natural pause at the top and bottom of each breath, and evening out the rate of inhalation and exhalation.

Try it now.

Really fill your lungs and then expel the breath. Even out your breathing as much as possible, without trying too hard. A more even breathing pattern will come with practice, over time.

Now imagine there is a still place at your core, in the middle of your body. This should be near your center of gravity, somewhere between your navel and your pelvic bowl. Take a breath. Allow your attention to drop into this center. Take a breath or two down here.

Now take another breath into your center. Imagine that your exhalation can move out in a line toward the edge of your energetic field, sometimes called your Shining Body, or the aura. Imagine that this breath can trace the edges of your field, down in front, under your feet, up in back, and over your head. Allow your awareness to notice both your center and your circumference, your core and your edge.

When we practice daily awareness of center and circumference, we gain all that we need to navigate our lives well. We have a compass and a sense of direction all around us. We also have a way to be fully present in the middle of it all.

Practice this exercise every day until you can get it down to three breaths. Breathe into center. Exhale and let attention drop. Breathe into center. Exhale to the outer edge of your Shining Body. Then breathe into center and just be. Once you can do this, the practice is always available to you, if you choose to continue to use it.

Do this practice every time you begin your mantra or sigil work and it will serve you well. Your magic will gain focus, clarity and power.

Do this practice every time you begin sit to write or rise to dance. Invoke the spirit of creativity into your presence and let the creative process that is always unfolding in the cosmos flow through the point of flesh and light that is you, unique in time. Right now.

To Fly: the Arrow

I made this sigil to help keep my aim in mind. It can be used in a bind-sigil for bigger projects (we'll discuss those later) but is really useful to invoke for hitting your daily or session targets. The arrow says, "go this way." In other words, don't dawdle, and certainly don't move back. Don't spend your productivity session noodling around, daydreaming, or making up excuses for why you can't do what you set out to do today. This is a great focus rune that reminds us we have one goal for this particular session and all of our energy and attention is going toward that. Right now.

To Work: Lamed

The Ox Goad. This sigil is also the first letter in the Hebrew word "to learn." Lamed keeps our will in line with the task of production. Getting the ox moving signals that we are ready to harness our power to do. It's not much use having a powerhouse of an animal if it sits in the shade day after day. The ox's power diminishes if it doesn't work—whether that work is for itself or for the person plowing the field is up to whatever arrangement is made between them. We can and should treat our ox well, and forming an agreement with it ensures the necessary work gets done. Draw upon Lamed when you need to stay the course.

Cleansing and Clearing

To do any sort of magic, it is helpful to be as clean and clear as possible. We want to be clear in our intention, in our energy, in our emotions, and in our lives.

Remember though, we can't wait until we feel "perfect" to do our work, whether that is magic, or writing, or anything else. So I'll repeat: it is helpful to be as clean and clear *as possible* in this moment.

We don't wait for the right moment; we make the best of the moment we have. That isn't to say that for acts of magic, timing doesn't matter. It can and it does. But the daily ins and outs of both creative practice and spiritual practice are what matter the most. Showing up daily to the altar, the notebook, the computer, the dance floor, or the canvas keeps us in the flow and enables us to already be up to speed when we need to make a big push. Whether we are meeting a hard deadline, or the right phase of the moon, advance preparation supports our intention every time.

When is the best time to do a clearing? Every day.

Align yourself. Center yourself. Clear your energy fields and your mind. Slow your breathing down and be with the sources of your creative spirit.

When is the best time to do a *big* clearing? When there is acute need is one good time. Otherwise, it is traditional to use the time of the waning moon, when it is heading back toward dark. That way, should we want to do a big working to charge up a sigil or a spell to help us, we are ready when the waxing moon comes back into view in the sky.

What do we clear?

- What we think other's expectations of us are.
- Our fears of failure or success.
- Distractions.
- Grandiose fantasies that keep us from doing the work.
- Anything else that keeps us from creative success.

How do we clear?

- Incense or smudge.
- Sound: toning, bells, or singing bowls.
- Salt scrub in the shower.
- The Rite of Unbinding (explained below).
- Aura Clearing Breath (explained below).

The other thing I want to mention about clearing and cleansing is that our ordinary lives are not dirty, profane things that need to be scrubbed clean before any "sacred" work can be done. All we are doing in these sorts of clearings is making more space. The more space we have inside, the more clarity is available to us.

Think of it: If your brain is cluttered with constant worry, how does that affect your creativity? If your working space is covered with piles of stuff, how much longer does it take you to find the tools you need? We don't need sterility and complete order—those can also impede our connection to art—but we do need to not be completely weighed down or buried.

Find your favorite ways to cleanse and clear and make some space and time to do both. Your creative life will thank you.

The Rite of Unbinding

This rite has many forms that I've been taught, and have practiced, and passed along over the years. I got it from the Anderson Feri Tradition. It is a simple rite done with a cup of water and is used to start the process of untying some of the knots within us that have become tighter and more tangled over the years. These can be knots from ill health, anxiety, or fear; knots of thinking we know all the answers; or knots of wishing for perfection; knots of things we need to forgive ourselves or others for…on and on. The list is legion.

The Rite of Unbinding is not an instant healing technique, nor will it clear everything away at once. What it does is enables us to loosen all the things that bind our hearts and souls and keep us from a clear flow of life energy.

All you need for this rite is a cup with a couple of inches of water in it, your attention, and your breath.

If you work with a God or Goddess, now would be a good time to call on them for help. Also, call upon your own divine nature to be present with you now. Call your animal and human natures, too. Ask all of yourself to be present and working together.

Action

What feels like it is binding you up today? If you can't name it, that is all right, too. Focus on that. Then begin to slow and regulate your breathing. It helps to gently touch the tip of your tongue to the front edge of your soft palette. Imagine that as you breathe, you are filling up with life and light. Imagine this breath of life and light filling every cell and pushing its way out toward your skin. Feel the life and light pushing out through your skin, out into the energy fields around you, filling you. Take as much time as you need. As you breathe, imagine that breath, life, and light begins loosening the knots that bind you. Imagine the released energy—all that which needs healing, forgiveness, or hope—flowing down your arms and into your hands. Place your hands over the cup of water and allow the bound-up energy, pushed by breath, life, and light, to fill the water of the cup until it glows, luminous, in your imagination.

Once you feel filled up, inside and out, with breath, life, and light, and once the process of unbinding feels completed for today, imagine that this energy flowing through and from you continues to flow into the cup of water, charging it up.

Say a prayer inside yourself now, to your own God Soul, to your deity, or to the cosmos. Ask for a blessing of good health and liberation. Take in a deep breath and release it with a humming sound toward the water.

This water, and that which was once bound up in you, is now blessed. Take in another breath and then drink the water down without stopping.

That which was bound up in you is now free, sending healing and blessing throughout you as the water assimilates itself into your body once again.

Aura Clearing Breath

I developed this exercise to help clear things we are carrying that don't feel like our own. Many creatives carry the expectations or opinions—perceived or real—of others inside our heads. These can stunt creativity and cause us to talk about things like "writer's block," which is really just a term we use instead of talking about our insecurity and fear.

We can also carry worry for others. The need to caretake others. The feeling that if we take time to create, we are stealing time from someone else.

Creatives can carry a lot. The more we carry, the less energy we have to create.

Take a moment and let it sink in that everything we are carrying that is related to someone else's words, opinions, needs, or perceived thoughts or responses doesn't have to be carried by us. They simply are not ours to carry, whether they've been put upon us by other people or situations or whether we've taken them on willingly ourselves. To carry those responsibilities for other adult humans is to disrespect their own autonomy and to hinders our own. If we have commitments to small children or infirm elders, for example, we may need to negotiate the very real responsibilities we have in order to carve out creative time. It isn't a bad idea even in these cases to notice whether we have taken on more than we need to.

Carry what it is honorable to carry, and no more. Don't diminish other people by over-caretaking

Let your creative process stand on its own two feet. Metaphorically, of course.

Action

Take a deep breath. That's where all of our magic begins. Breathe into your center, that place between your navel and your pelvis. Settle in.

Let it be your intention that you clear your energy fields of anything you are currently carrying that isn't yours to carry. Breathe into center and exhale with a powerful "whoosh!" Imagine that your breath pushes everything out of your field that isn't yours. Do this three times.

Take a fourth breath and imagine your exhalation tracing the outer edge of your energy field, redefining your boundary, and re-setting your space.

Remain for awhile with this sense of who you are beneath other's worries, needs, opinions, or expectations.

In this place, what would you like to create?

The Art of Commitment

Words of Power

As people who want to more effectively tap or support our creativity, why is magic useful to us again?

Sometimes our creativity needs a boost. We might need help with inspiration. Or to motivate ourselves toward more production. Or with getting our work out into the world. Or bringing more money in to support our lives so we can continue to do the work we desire to do.

Mantras and sigils can help with any of these.

Whenever I do a soul reading for a client, I always close by giving them a mantra to use. I tune us back in and find the essence of the reading, encapsulated in a simple phrase. After offering it to the client, I ask them to say the phrase out loud, three times, every time I ring a singing bowl. The combination of the bowl resounding and the person saying the mantra out loud helps to seed the reading further into the person *and* communicates this essence to the cosmos. The reading becomes, then, not just a reading, but an act of magic that helps to carry the person forward.

Hearing the words spoken aloud in their own voice is important.

Repeating the phrase three times is important.

The querent becomes more than a client in that moment: they take the reins and become the charioteer, driving forward, aligned with their own will. Using the mantra becomes an act of magic. Though they came to me for guidance, they leave knowing that continuing to shape the future is in their hands, hearts, and voice.

Mantras are used to shift our consciousness as well. Traditionally, they are used to connect us—via word and sound—to what is sacred. Mantras are prayers that remind us to open to a broader sense of the world. Things exist that can kindle awe, take our breath away, or inspire us beyond all reason.

That is an important phrase: *beyond all reason.* Although making art requires input from our minds, the art and design that hooks us, transforming us, even if only for a moment, is not reasonable. The writer or artist risked something in order to communicate the experience that took us over.

Think back on dancing to live music, and the moment where the band, the lights, and the crowd all came together and filled you with a mighty rush. Think on turning the corner in a museum and seeing a painting that makes you want to stand in front of it for an hour. Think on the stories that have stayed with you. Or the poem that changed your mind. These all tapped something un-reasonable within you.

While we need our wonderful minds to help us plan, to set things up, to remember our training or the proper information, we also need help letting go of reason. To do otherwise is to let our critical selves run the creative process. That is the surest way to derail the sacred upwelling of creation longing to be shared. We need to speak the unreasonable words out loud, and ring a sacred bell, sending ripples moving all directions: inside and out, as above reflecting as below.

A mantra is a sacred utterance. An utterance of power. It is more than an affirmation—it is an invocation. By insisting that our creativity is sacred, we honor our process and begin to invoke our own success. By speaking the mantra, again and again, we free something inside us that is otherwise bound by conventions and reason. All protestations of the "this is the way it is done" get shaken from their moorings and what is unusual steps forth.

Words have power and we should put power behind our words. What risk is it to say a prayer? On one hand, the risk is small: it takes a few moments of our full attention. On the other hand, it is a great risk, because we may just call the things we want and need into our lives.

This is a risk: To light a candle and say to ourselves or our Gods, "I invoke the will to create."

This is a risk: To say, "I call upon the support I need to do this holy work."

This is a risk: To utter the words, "I call a better life to me."

This is a risk: To say, really say, to the cosmos, "I wish my work to spread, to be successful, and to plant the seeds I desire."

A prayer can be either an invocation or an evocation.

A spell can help us to draw things toward us.

To invoke is to draw something down and in. To infuse a person, place, or object with sacred power. We repeat our sacred phrases to help draw the power down.

To evoke is to draw forth and out. To fill space with what we are calling.

Action

I ask again:

What do you want? What do you need?
What do you desire?

Write that down. Now write it again in the form of a sacred utterance, or an invocation. What do you want to draw in? What is the phrase that will enable you to have the success you desire?

Whether that success is "My writing will communicate clearly."

or

"I am in the creative flow."

or

"My words will enter the world like tongues of flame."

or

"I will have success."

Then decide:

Do I wish to invoke or evoke? To call in or draw forth?

For the purposes of charging up sigils or objects, I suggest invocation. An invocation will spread as the sigil spreads, causing the intention to also be evoked out into the world. Or I can invoke into a talisman in order to continue focusing my will and intention.

We will cover this further when we talk about sigils and talismans.

For the purposes of drawing a certain quality out of myself or the work I'm doing, I want to evoke. If I wish the painting or music set to instill a certain quality in the space or the audience, I want to evoke that quality from the work and into the space or the people gathered there. At other times, I may wish to evoke something from myself that I've had trouble tapping into. It might be a deeper truth, a richer sense of desire, or even some difficult emotional states that need to be communicated to make one of my characters have greater depth, or to give the music or drawing a deeper connection to human truth.

So I ask myself: What is the essence I want reflected in the work; how can I fill and surround myself with the power of my intention? What do I need to call in, and what do I need to draw forth?

Our prayers and spells are shaped by our answers to these questions.

The Dawn: Dagaz

Daybreak. This is the rune of new light. The rune of beginning again. Dawn is on the horizon, bridging day and night. Dagaz is a great rune for will development because of the sheer *dailyness* of it. Every single day we get a chance to re-commit to our creative tasks. Every time we re-commit, our will increases. Every time our will increases, so does our ability to create. Didn't meet your commitment yesterday? That's just fine, because you can fulfill your promise to yourself today. When we invoke daily commitment, our work has the opportunity to go far. We are able to craft our success, simply by showing up every time the sun rises.

The Anvil

The anvil is the place where tools are made, and new shapes come into form from raw materials. Sometimes, in order to develop our own wills, we need to place ourselves between the hammer and the anvil, allowing heart and soul to be shaped into a creative tool. The anvil is a platform for work. It is also the place where all of the blacksmith's skill comes into play. For those of us staring at a blank page or an empty canvas, the anvil is a marvelous metaphor: the anvil invokes our ability to take imagination, skill, and talent and join these with the materials of our craft. Writers hammer out their stories. Dancers forge new movements. Composers strike notes together, making a new song.

Signatures and Symbols

Pause for a moment and think about how amazing language actually is. We've codified a series of sounds into groupings and given them meaning and significance. We have then taken that a step further and figured out how to transmit that meaning even when we are absent from one another. That is some marvelous combination of science, art, craft, and magic.

Not only can we speak of things that we experience in the world, we can also speak of things that exist only in the imagination, in possibility. Language allows us a vast capacity to dream. From these dreams come new creations.

To name something that doesn't yet exist in manifest form is the first step toward making it real. There is a reason that in Kabbalah, the sphere of dream and imagination is often named "Foundation." This reflects Plato's idea that there is a place where Forms exist, before they even show up here on earth. There is a sense of divine imagination as being a real force, with effect. For a creative, that alone is a powerful concept.

Imagination makes creation possible. Imagination is, therefore, part of reality. When we are told to "be realistic" and to do something practical instead of creating art, we can respond, "I am realistic. I'm just in touch with a reality that doesn't yet exist."

That reality doesn't yet exist because we are in the process of bringing it into being. That is how all inventions are formed. What could be more practical than that?

So, we go on long walks in the woods or on city streets, or we take baths, or make cups of tea. We read books and look at paintings, and pipe music into our ears. All the while, our imagination is working, sometimes in the background, and sometimes in the fore. We start to tinker with what our imagination is bringing to us. At a certain point, we tinker long enough that these inchoate things coalesce enough that we can finally give them a name. A marker. Something that makes this process emerging from the imaginal realm more solid.

To name a thing is one way to help establish a relationship with it. A name is a link. A transmitter of information and energy. Words, names, and symbols help establish pathways between things.

Think of the first thing most of us do when we encounter someone that we've never seen before: we exchange names. Often this exchange is is coupled with clasping one another's hands. The exchange of names—an introduction of one person's marker to another—is now linked with a physical sense. We have a greater doorway into the other person than we had before this introduction.

A signature is a symbol for a name.

In order to invoke our creative desires, art requires some of us drag them up from the darkness where they have been gestating, toward the sun of consciousness. It is there that we must shake their hands and ask their names. Test their weight. Notice whether or not we feel a connection.

Some of us may need to do the converse: our desires have been occluded by too much brilliance, too much dazzle, busyness, longing, sound, and fury. We must pull them back toward shadowy, safe places, toward the sort of rest that heals us and allows our desires to become whole. Only then can we get to know them better, and get a sense of their *true* names—not their use names, which are simple placeholders for the real thing, and not the false names of fantasy or "someday" we've been giving our desires.

There are so many creatives—us—who never make time to write, or paint, or dance, or make music. Or if we try, we do so in a haphazard fashion, never dedicating any real time and attention to the process. Never allowing ourselves to practice, we too easily give up after a time—sometimes one year, sometimes ten—saying "I just can't make this work." Ten years of regular, dedicated relationship with our creative process is completely different than ten years of random, waiting-for-inspiration-to-strike or the-perfect-project-to-come-along relationship.

There comes a time when we need to ask ourselves what sort of relationship with creativity we actually have, and what sort of relationship we want.

Many of us also don't allow enough space for imagination to come forward, and enough space to get messy with it. We want imagination to be correct, instead of the nascent possibility that it is, shaped by its relationship with our minds, hearts, and efforts.

Some of us, of course, have dedicated ourselves to the relationship, and allow ourselves to play with imagination and with practicing our craft. We can use the help of magic, too.

All of us, no matter how we feel about our creativity, can use more or *different* kinds of support from time to time. So, let's continue with the work of this book:

Regardless of where we are in our creative processes or careers, I want us to start working with words regarding creative desire and success now. In this moment. These don't have to be the exact, right words that will form our sacred utterance, but, as with all acts of magic and creativity, we have to start somewhere. And we have to start some time.

Action

Return to your answers to these questions: What do I want? What do I need? What do I desire?

In looking over those answers, what stands out for you? What sets up a resonance in your body, a tugging at your belly or a humming in your heart?

Is there a key sense or feeling rising inside of you?
How would you express that?

Write it down. Write it down as fully as you can: one paragraph, or one page.

Then, breathe again. Invoke your Gods or spirits if you wish to. Read your words again.

Return to the work we did in our last section and ask:

Do I want to invoke or evoke? Draw in, or bring forth?

Answer that question, as best you can. Again, this answer is just for right now, not forever. We get to practice magic just as we practice writing stories or going up and down our scales.

Sit with your words. Drop into your center. Ask for guidance. Ask to be shown:

What do I desire? What would help my creativity?
What does success look like for me?

Then start to pare down the non-essentials. Try to get your page down to a paragraph, or your paragraph down to a sentence or two.

What we'll do with this next is begin to practice honing our will in relationship to our desire.

Ready?

Charging Our Intention

All desires have an essential nature, a kernel. A core.

To hone something is to pare it down to essence.

If our desire is too vast, heart and soul can become confused. Mind and body, too. Where do we begin? How will we ever get there?

We've honed our page or paragraph down. Look at what you've written in answer to the questions regarding your creative desire. Does it *feel* right? Is it too much? Too big or scattered? Or is it not enough?

Drop back into your center on a breath. Let your attention sink. Try to get a clearer sense of your connection to what you've noted down so far.

If it doesn't feel quite right, look for the heart of it. You may need to write something fresh. This time, limit yourself to three sentences, maximum.

Tinker for awhile.

Perhaps you need to do a cleansing—I've written about cleansings in their own section.

The thing I suggest at this phase is this: don't tinker too long. That may cause your perfectionist or your inner critic to emerge. Don't engage with this process for more than three days. If you've gone that long, buckle down and say "This is what I *choose*, right or wrong." To follow desire, we must risk. Every choice is a risk, even when we think we are not choosing.

Once you have honed the statement of your desire down to something simpler—a feeling, an image, a phrase—it is time to begin using it as a mantra.

Please risk doing this. Don't just read about it and pass it by. Recitation of words out loud does change something in us. Chanting or recitation helps build energy and also helps us figure out more clearly what we want.

This sacred phrase is well on its way to becoming our intention. Strong intentions are the basis for effective actions. We'll see how to hook them up with our will in a few sections, but I want us to get better acquainted with these mantras first.

Take a breath and take a risk by committing to the following piece of magic, which will charge up the wishes we've been working with and begin to set them as intentions that can work with us as we write, or dance, or paint, or create the lives we desire.

Action

Set up an altar space. It can be as simple as a candle on a table, or a stone you hold in your hand. Stand or sit as you wish. Make sure you are able to let your spine rise up from your pelvis in alignment with your skull to the best of your body's ability. If seated, it is useful to make sure your knees are below your hips.

Slow your breathing down. Pick whatever feels right as a physical anchor: light the candle or some incense, or hold the stone in whichever hand feels right. The candle or stone are simply ways to engage the body further, like the handshake when you first learn someone's name. We want that bridge, that sensory connection to our sacred word or phrase.

We want to get to know desire on as many levels as possible.

We want to open to the flow of creativity with every part of our self. We want to taste creativity. Smell creativity. Feel it. Hear it. See it. We want to connect to creative desire with as many senses as we have available to us.

Now, begin to recite the word or phrase out loud. Softly at first. Allow it to become rhythmic. Your body may wish to rock back and forth or side to side, or you may find yourself sitting completely still, aligned with the words, the sound, and the candle, incense, or stone.

Let your voice grow louder. Feel the sound rippling out around you, filling space with its vibration. Feel the link you have to creative desire grow inside you, and seed the world around you.

This is your first statement to the cosmos that "I will create. I will connect. And in creating, I call up my own success."

You've introduced yourself to your creative desire, and then introduced that desire to the inner ear of the cosmos, and your Gods.

Next, it is time to bring that creative intention into action, and further learn to engage your will.

The first step toward success
is deciding we want
to make a commitment.

Sigils Are Everywhere

Sigils communicate intention.

How much attention do you pay to logos? How often have you turned over a silver teapot in a thrift store to see if there was a maker's mark? What brands do you recognize simply by catching a glimpse of a color or a shape?

Every brand is a sigil. Every maker's mark is the same. Maker's marks are the "stamp of approval and authenticity" that carry the weight of the maker herself. A seal stands in for the person who *sets* the seal, whether onto metal or parchment.

Every time we sign something, we have the ability to enact magic. All we need to do is pay attention to that fact, center ourselves, and add a breath of power and intention to the signature, whether we are typing our name onto a finished manuscript, or signing the corner of a canvas.

All of these symbols carry in them the seeds of something, be it the our personal approval or a representation of a mission statement. From corporate brands, to an artisan's maker's mark, to signing our own names—there should be intention behind all of these sigils.

The same is true of the other sigils we are talking about. All sigils carry our work out into the world. They announce our presence and our intention without us having to be physically present. Their goal is to propagate and amplify our intentions, and to help us focus our will and keep our intention moving with the flow of life and creative juice.

I'm saying all of this to remind us that sigils are both magical and ordinary. They are used every day, all over the world, and have been for millennia. What makes our use of sigils unique is that it is our job to remember to infuse them with the magic that we want them to carry. These aren't just bold symbols; rather, they are representatives and ambassadors of our creative desire.

Other symbol forms we use every day are embedded in what I've mentioned already: alphabets. Letters represent sounds carried through the air, linking to thoughts. Some letters even have their own meaning apart from the words they form. Certain cultures consider letters to be made of light, or fire. That is how potent alphabets are.

Let's consider these alphabets for a second. People form sounds in order to communicate. Those sounds form words, offering more precise indications of meaning. We have taken these sounds and made glyphs of them so we can communicate with one another even when we are far distant in space and even time.

You are reading the coded symbols I've typed into a computer long after I had the thought that put them together. Alphabets, like all symbolic signatures, help us to travel through space and time, carrying encoded intentions. All symbols can be decoded in this way, if we stop to pay attention.

There are several alphabets that magic workers use to convey their sacred intention. Hebrew, Norse Runes, and Irish Oghams are all very useful alphabets, because each glyph has its own meaning. Chinese alphabets are the same. So these letters do double duty: making up words and conveying sound and thought, but also encapsulating a meaning all on their own. But people all over the world use all kinds of alphabets for magic: Roman letters, Cyrillic, Ancient Greek, Theban. Pretty much any alphabet you can name can be used to set intention.

The thing I find most useful about alphabet systems such as runes is the ease with which several meaning components can be combined with a few strokes of a

pen on paper, or a stylus on copper or wax. These com-
binations are known as "bindrunes" and are a type of
sigil work I've used off and on for years.

For example, if I wanted to focus on making money
from my writing and having a clear and open channel
for listening and conveying words, I might set out to
combine Fehu and Ansuz. Fehu is the rune shape taken
from cattle, often meaning "moveable wealth." Ansuz
is Odin's rune, the rune of listening for inspiration and
then speaking from the same.

When I start to work with these runes, I see that one
way of combining them lends itself to mirroring. Once
mirrored, other helpful runes emerge: Kenaz, the torch
made by human hands, that lights the way. Gebo, the
gift of equal exchange, which is another great rune for
creativity. There is also Elhaz, or elk sedge, a very sharp
reed often seen as a symbol of protection. I may want to
work with that in order to protect my writing time. So
you see, just by beginning to work with the runes and
create a combined form, many other meanings come
forward to help me from within the sigil pattern as it
forms. I can charge them all up with my breath, chanting, and intention, and find the support that I need.

The same runes could be combined differently, and
yet another meaning would emerge. What if I were to
draw them mirrored, facing one another? The two Fehus

and Ansuzs would then form the diamond shape of Ingwaz, the rune of Freyr, who is great to call upon for money, food, home, and sex; in other words, all good, solid life things that a writer or artist really needs. This shape also forms a nice road toward our goal.

Alchemical symbols can also be useful sigils for creativity. Just as I re-arrange the physical tools upon my altar according to what energies need structuring, balancing, or opening, we can call upon the symbols of fire, water, earth, air, and aether to evoke things within us, or to infuse our creative practice with some of the qualities of those elements. We might also consider using the symbol for the sun if we want our work brought further into the light, or we might invoke the power of the moon to instill our work with a deeper sense of mystery and a connection to the things that shine in darkness.

When it comes time for you to decide which sigils to use, I would ask which ones sing to you, and which you gravitate toward. If you've never worked with Oghams, for example, but they tug at you, start working with them as sigils while simultaneously engaging in study of the system itself.

I did this with runes. I began working with a few runes for specific purposes because, after years of using Tarot cards, I was gravitating away from that for divination and was doing readings for others solely based on my own combination of psychic and intuitive skills. But, regarding *personal* insight, occasionally I wanted a more pointed reading to answer questions and to get input from the parts of me that weren't "pinging" intuitively or via my guides. Runes stepped forward to offer themselves. So as I started using a handful for specific workings, and took it upon myself to study one rune every day as part of my spiritual practice. This was very helpful and though I am no means a rune master, I now have enough of an ongoing relationship with the system that I can make bindrunes with ease.

The same is not true for the Hebrew alphabet or the Oghams. I have a very cursory knowledge of both, and checked in with colleagues who have deep, ongoing relationships with these systems to make sure I was on the right track when presenting the few I use as examples in this book.

The more resonance we have with a system, the more resonance the magic will have. That is both my experience and my opinion. Other magicians may disagree with me on this. Some of them chant in foreign languages they don't know specifically to keep things as abstract as possible in order to let go of attachment to the outcome of the operation. That doesn't work for me. I want to honor the systems by knowing them before asking them to work for me. Just as I wouldn't pull a

Goddess out of a hat and expect her to help me with a piece of magic, I don't use sacred letters that way.

What I recommend is trying things out and seeing what works for you.

Remember, you can always make your own sigils, which can communicate your intention to all the parts of your soul and to the cosmos. While there is one sort of power that comes from using an alphabet that has been charged up through use by other humans for millennia, there is a different sort of power that arises from using something fresh, something that bears your imprint alone. That is the beauty of maker's marks and brands: they use familiar forms in unique ways, which creates a synergy all its own.

There are several alphabets and sigil systems at the end of this book. You may wish to take a moment to look at them now.

Working With Bindrunes

Fehu and Ansuz

Fehu is the rune for cattle, or moveable wealth. It helps me to invoke financial success from my writing. Ansuz is Odin's rune, the rune of divine inspiration, of listening and speaking within the flow of all creation.

Below are two examples of joining them, forming a combined sigil known as a bindrune.

Developing Our Will

Sigils and mantras can only help us if we let them.

In order to create, we must be willing to do so. Willingness is openness. Willingness says either, "I will open myself to this unfamiliar experience," or it says "I will take action to follow up on either my promises or my desire."

Habits can either bolster our willingness or tear it down.

Our magic begins every day, with the first things we choose to do.

If I'm in the habit of getting out of bed upon waking and doing some practices that center me, and then sitting down to write with a cup of tea, that shows my willingness to create. This habit bolsters my will. If, on the other hand, upon waking, I check in on Facebook, or immediately start answering e-mails in order to put out fires that arose in the night, I signal that I'm not in touch with a willingness to write, or paint, or engage in other creative acts. My wish to create is just a thought, not backed up by action. I have no will to create.

No matter when we schedule our creative time, what we do in the morning is key to our success. I've found with myself, my clients, and my students, that setting the tone for the day influences all of our other actions. So, even if our creative time is late at night, after our household has quieted down, we are well served by getting out of bed and centering ourselves upon waking. Perhaps this means connecting with body and breath, or with prayer, or some other activity that allows us to enter our day with clarity and attention instead of scattered and on the run.

Those of you without homes who may be reading this: I trust that you will adapt my language in a way that makes sense to your current situation, be you in a shelter, on a friend's couch, or on the streets.

Choose that which supports your wish to be present to creativity throughout the day, no matter how busy your calendar is, and no matter what pressures you are currently living under. Creativity is important.

Will sets our intentions into action. We apply ourselves to the actions that bring desire into focus and then toward manifestation. As long as we keep saying we want something and not changing our habits to support this, we continue to undermine our will and diminish our effectiveness.

One step toward increasing our will toward creative success is learning to distinguish fantasy from desire. I describe fantasy as a way to try on different hats and see which ones look or feel right. But as a way to try things out, or as temporary respite from stress, is all that fantasy is good for. Fantasy used as an escape strategy is only temporarily useful to us. Sometimes we need a metaphorical cookie, and that is just fine. However, if we are constantly escaping instead of learning to apply will, we will never have creative success.

Desire is not fantasy. Desire is the place where want and need meet, and we become *willing*, oftentimes at great cost, to do what it takes to fulfill our deep, soul longing.

The creative impulse is the impulse toward desire.

When we have a creative impulse—when we say, "I want to write" or "I want to dance"—we are honoring the life force rising up inside us. This life force connects us to the sun, the soil, the breeze, the rain, and the stars.

Creativity connects us to all of life. Creativity links us to the unfolding dance of the cosmos.

In order to create, we must move from saying "I want" to saying "I will." We must set an intention and then act upon it, and we do this with as much consistency as possible.

We begin where we are: with whatever amount of time and energy we have. Beginning where we are enable us to continue. Continuing increases the flow of life force.

The open secret of magic and will development is that the more consistently we step into even the smallest flow, the easier it becomes. Over time, the small flow of life, creativity, and magic only increases. But the increase happens the way water widens a channel in rock or sand: it only happens by steady application.

Will harnesses life force and life force feeds our will. What supports this? The smallest daily practice helps. Showing up. Committing to ourselves and to our writing or our other creative tasks.

Believe it or not, intermittent creativity—"waiting for inspiration to strike"—is much more difficult than steady application, over time. When we await inspiration, we are starting cold every time, and having to re-learn everything we know. This also tends to leave us flat when the initial surge is over. When we show up regularly, whether that is three times a week, or every day, all the parts of ourselves learn to get on board. "This is what we do on Tuesday, Thursday, and Saturday afternoons. Okay. We're ready!" Just like a dog knows it gets a walk when its person gets home, our creative parts know when it is time to get to work, as long as we establish a routine.

Every time we show up for our creative appointments, our will increases, and so does our access to steady creative flow.

And that includes the days when "I don't feel like it" is the phrase of the moment. It doesn't matter. Do it anyway. You may not get your word count in, but you'll get something done, and best of all, you'll stay in training, which is as important for an author or artist as it is for an athlete.

The Oak: Dair

When I think of strength, oak always stands out for me. Sturdy. Stable. Oak stands its ground. It is a hardwood and is used to make things that last, as well. So, for calling on the energy of steady application, Oak is a great way to go. Oak endures over time. Oak also stands out, which is all the better for successful creative endeavors. We want confidence in our strength, and we want our creative work to be seen, heard, and felt by others. For steady strength and long-lasting effects, Oak is our ally. When we need the confidence to stand tall in our work, invoking Oak lends us a stronger spine.

The Ox: Aleph

The first letter of the Hebrew alphabet, this one letter represents the whole. Aleph is also known as "the Ox," which represents our strength and fortitude. Our ability to go forth, even when it feels difficult—even when we feel weary, or the sun is high in the sky, or the soil is filled with rocks. The field must be plowed in order to yield food. The words must be written in order for the story to be told. The Ox does well when it has food, rest, shelter, *and* is exercised regularly. The more regular the exercise, the more amenable the Ox is to do the necessary work. This sigil can also be effectively used with Lamed, the Ox Goad.

Setting Our Goals

I want us to work with goals and intentions to invoke creative success. And...

Working with goals and intentions can seem straightforward, but until we make two subtle shifts in our minds, these can also trip us up, leading us into delusion, frustration, or wheel-spinning.

The first shift comes from a primary rule of all magic: the outcome is never going to look exactly the way we thought it would. Every magic worker who's been practicing for any length of time figures out that once we make a move, the future changes. First of all, we've introduced an action that didn't exist before. Of course that changes things. Second, the cosmos is made up of many shifting, interlocking parts, many of which have their own sentience, opinions, and agendas. So having "I'm going to write a bestselling book" as our goal or intention is pretty much useless. It's bad magic.

Bad magic assumes that we control the cosmos. We simply do not. All we can do is make our very best attempts to follow up on the things we *can* control. We can ask for greater inspiration, and then find ways to be more open to it in our lives. We can say, "I will write five days a week" and then calendar the time, using a sigil as a magical reminder that writing five days a week is our aim. We can set "I will write a book" as our intention and then figure out what our target word count is, divide that by 250 (for words per page) and then figure out what writing pace we want to set for ourselves.

Magic can boost any of these goals, and more. Magic can help keep us inspired, focused, and paying attention to our relationship with art and with the process of learning our craft. What magic cannot do is what *we* cannot do: control the world.

We can't control art galleries, but we can keep studying and painting, and figuring out the business. We can't control who buys our books, but we can do our utmost to make sure our books are the best ones we can write, and that they get proper editing and an eye-catching cover. And we can study the publishing or music business—traditional or indie—to find out what methods seem to work best to boost sales and reach, and then tailor our will and magical operations toward some of those goals.

And no matter what we do, the outcome should still surprise us, because that is how magic works. I thank the Gods for that. What a boring world it would be if I knew exactly what was going to happen all the time. I want to work hard, to set clear intentions, and then I want to see how the world meets me.

Allowing the world to meet us is important because micromanaging our magic, even when it is successful, can have less than stellar consequences. Even if the outcome is pretty darned close to the initial goal we set, we may find ourselves too blocked in and constrained by it. This then tilts toward the opposite of Dean Wesley Smith's "failure to success" and becomes a "success to failure."

One great example of "success to failure" is illustrated in the book *Art and Fear*: an artist's only goal was to have a one-person show at Gallery X. They worked really hard and finally, one day, their one-person show at Gallery X opened. They had achieved success! That artist never painted again.

Why is that? Their goals had nothing to do with their inner landscape, their relationship to their art, or to their *process* of making art. Their goal had only to do with this one gallery and what a one-person show represented. That success was highly symbolic, it meant something to the artist; likely what it meant is "I've made it!" And once we've "made it," our process stops.

"Making it" is deadly to all acts of creativity and invention.

A writer or artist in tune with their desires knows that symbols of success are symbols only. A desire with greater longevity is this: to keep learning and creating and sharing our work for as long as we take breath, or until it ceases to be interesting to us. Then we set out to learn and do something new.

So, that was the first shift of mind: recognizing that the outcome of our goals won't turn out exactly the way we thought when we began. We'll return to this topic in another section, but first I want to address the second shift of mind necessary for building effective magic:

It is best to be clear in our intentions, but not too concrete. We need to find a way to state our desires clearly without dictating the particulars. What do I mean by this?

Let's take this out of the realm of art for a moment. If I was looking for a new job, I would not create a spell that encapsulates the message, "I will get this position at that company with this salary." Why not? Isn't that clear? Well, it *is* clear, but it is also the equivalent of saying "I will write a bestseller." We can't actually *will* either. There are too many factors out of our control. Also, what if the immediate supervisor at that company turns out to be a terrible person to work for? Or what if they would have offered us more money, if only we had asked? Or what if a job much better suited to our skills was just around the corner, but we didn't even look at it because we were fixated on one particular job?

What I have found most effective is to tell ourselves and the cosmos *exactly* what we want to manifest in this way: "I seek a position where I will feel happy and challenged, in a company that respects my skills and talents and will pay me very well." This sets our attitude and energy around the job search, tells the universe what we want, and leaves room for the universe to meet us, and work its own magic. We are not in this alone. There is, at best, reciprocity in magic and in art.

So in crafting an intention, the specificity we want to work toward is claiming the emotions, and sensations, and the context for our satisfaction, success, and joy.

Set a goal. State your intention. Then let the cosmos do its own creative work.

Customizing Our Sigils

One common way of forming a sigil is something I learned from Chaos Magic practitioners. This is the method of crossing out. There are various ways to do this. The most basic is to take the magical phrase you've begun working with and turn it into a symbol.

Here is an example:

"I am open to the inspiration from the cosmos
and enter the creative flow."

What I want to do is first cross out any repeating letters, leaving only single letters:

"I am open t/ /h/ i/s//r///// f/ /// c///// //d ///// /// /////v/ /l/w."

This leaves us with "I am open thsrfcdvlw." We have several options now. Some people cross out all the vowels, leaving only consonants. You may wish to try that method.

One way I would work with this is to start making shapes of the letters, drawing them over one another, seeing how they fit together, and whether or not they share any lines or curved borders.

That is one way to work with the phrase. Another way would be to notice the fact that when we started crossing out letters, an intact phrase remained: "I am open." That feels significant to me. One thing we could do, then, is to start making a symbol just from those three words, knowing that they include the intention of the whole.

Turn to the next section, "Sigilized Intentions," for visuals of both of these processes.

You'll see that in the second example, I ended up working with the words "I am" coupled with a symbol of openness. I experimented with a few shapes—a door, a circle—before settling on an arrow as the simplest way to convey a sense of opening something. I was thinking of how infographics use arrows to show the direction a door or window opens in case of emergency. I wanted the arrow to move in a forward direction, moving from present into future, rather than pointing toward the past.

The key here is to take the sentence—"I am open to the inspiration from the cosmos and enter the creative flow"—and turn it into an abstraction, a signature, a symbol of itself. We want a magical shape that will encapsulate the essence of the phrase. My preference is always for clean, geometric, graphic representation, but many magicians like to turn the abstraction into a creature, animating that figure with intention. Artist Grant Morrison famously put his creature-ized sigils into his comic books so the magic would continue to work every time someone bought or borrowed the book and opened to that page.

Take your sentence and start playing with this method. See what happens. Allow yourself to let go of preconceptions about beauty and form. Allow intuition to drive the bus. Call upon your creativity to help you in this process.

If you find you keep getting stuck, tripping yourself up on making sure the sigil looks "just right," then I recommend returning to the Cleansing and Clearing exercises. Perhaps your work space needs clearing, or perhaps your own energy field does. Feeling stuck is sometimes our intuition telling us to pay attention to something, but in the midst of creation, it is more often that we are worried about a lack of perfection. You may wish to skip ahead and read that section, too.

This crossing-out method is only one way to work our magical phrase or mantra into a sigil to help our work. I've used that method with success and feel it taught me a great deal about getting to the essence of my desire in order to activate my magic. Those lessons have served me well and brought me to the sigil method I use most often these days, when I'm not using runes: I create sigils based on my own intuition of what feels potent and true.

I'll give you one example. When I recommitted myself to writing fiction, I knew I needed to power up my ability to practice, learn, and produce. I wanted to charge up a candle and activate a mantra to work with. As we've been discussing so far, I came up with the magical phrase first, after some visioning, listening, pulling some runes, and paring things down.

The phrase I came up with was "Words Light Worlds." I wanted my writing to inspire me and to spread like little sparks of light throughout the whole World Tree. At least, that is what I recall of that initial magical operation. It was three years before this writing and as we know, spells alter over time. I anointed an orange candle with oil. I carved runes that symbolized the spread of light—mainly Kenaz, the Torch. Then I began to work with that orange candle as I wrote. I would light the candle and invoke that mantra.

This led me to writing the first draft of a novel in August and September of 2013. That novel became *Like Water* and led to me founding my own publishing company. The novel was terribly timely. Its characters struggle with the aftermath of police violence, and one year after the first draft was written, Mike Brown was killed in Ferguson, Missouri, and the young people there refused to go home. Within that year, Alicia Garza and her friends came up with the phrase "Black Lives Matter" and, via a hashtag and a lot of on-the-ground persistence, a new movement was born.

In other words, I couldn't wait on the machine of traditional publishing to get the book out. I had set it aside in order to get more practice writing fiction. After years of publishing nonfiction books on spirituality with traditional publishers, I was apprenticing to the art of fiction once again. Still working with the mantra of "Words Light Worlds," I had set myself a task of writing one short story a week and begun taking writing classes that sharpened my abilities.

In the aftermath of Ferguson, *Like Water* came knocking on my door again, practically slamming it down. I did an editorial pass—because the book was written out of order, I had to see where the segments fit and what was missing—sent it to four first readers for impressions, did another pass to incorporate the feedback that made sense, and hired an editor.

Then I founded PF Publishing. All still using orange candles charged up with the mantra "Words Light Worlds." However, the simple Kenaz rune wasn't enough. It wasn't quite right to become the maker's mark of this new venture of spreading light and fire through the power of the written word.

So I worked with the mantra. I tinkered. I prayed. I tried things out and started again.

And in the midst of this process, the sigil for PF Publishing emerged, an elegant sweep of a flame. Easy. Simple. Spreadable.

I carved it on an orange candle and started burning it when working on the novel and when doing the tasks of setting up the publishing company.

That sigil gets charged up every time someone buys a book.

The symbol encapsulates the essence of my magical phrase. I didn't use the crossing-out method: I didn't need to. But years of using the crossing-out method helped me get to the point where forming a sigil like the PF logo became a relatively straightforward magical operation.

This flame now lights my way, imprinting itself onto every book that goes out into the world, taking my message, my magic, and my hopes with it. That flame also reminds me of the larger goals and intentions I'm working with regarding writing. The flame connects me to the Goddess Brigid, whom I work with on these projects every day, and with Prometheus, who stole fire from the Gods. It also lights a fire beneath me, powering the daily magics that support every step of my current writing career. The magic all works together as a whole: from the time I get out of bed in the morning, until I'm back in bed, book in my lap, ready to close my day.

The thing about this sort of magic is that we can allow it to become our companion. And good companions help to keep us on our way.

Sigilized Intentions

"I am open to the inspiration from the cosmos
and enter the creative flow."

"I am open thsrfcdvlw."

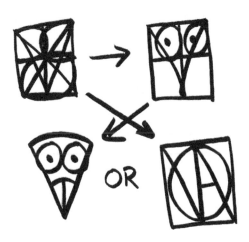

Here is the further simplified intention:

"I am open."

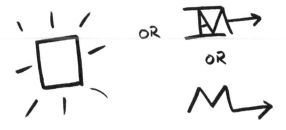

To Forget or Recall?

Some magic workers are of the opinion that once we've done a magical operation, we should try to forget all about it. Many magicians try to make their mantras and sigils so abstract that they don't even recall what the intention was behind them. They so much wish to release attachment to the outcome that they release the entire operation once it is done, allowing the magic to make its own way into the world.

There is merit to this thinking, and it is particularly good advice for those of us who continuously want to control and manage outcomes even when trying not to. Working in this way allows us to release attachment and allow the cosmos to step up as it will. This also gives greater rein to our subconscious, which may very well still be working on the project without our conscious knowledge.

I often do this with New Year's Eve intentions. I don't set a resolution, but I do set an intention, pulling runes for insight into the intention, and then speaking it aloud to my friends. We all do this in a round, before midnight strikes. That intention setting is powerful magic. Some years, I write it down and post it in my office as a reminder of my work for the year. More often, however, I leave the intention to work its way through my life, and don't look at it again until the following year, when it is time to set a new one. It's always surprising to see the ways in which the magic of New Year's has manifested over the course of the intervening year. I am helped to remain present with what is actually happening, rather than trying to make something happen. As someone who has worked very hard to develop follow-through and will, and as a person who thinks I "know the correct way" things should go, this is good magic.

That said, when doing sigil magic and mantra work, I often want to remain engaged. I tend to do some combination of paying attention and forgetting about the focus. I'll offer a couple of examples:

When doing big, life-altering spell work, I like to craft the spell over time, returning to it in different phases of the moon, crafting and refining the statement of my desire. Then I let the spell "rest," sometimes for one month, and sometimes for an entire quarter, after which I look at it again. If it still resonates, I see whether or not it needs a few adjustments. If the energy and desire still feel strong and true, I finish the spell, do a big magical working around it, and then release it. If I've distilled a mantra or sigil from the working, I will continue to work with that on a regular basis, but I let the particulars of the spell go.

What I've found from these sorts of workings is that the spell manifests things far greater and more marvelous than my imagination at the time could even comprehend. If I had been trying to micromanage the outcome, I would have limited the success of the spell. So for these spells, I both work with a distilled *essence* of the spell—via a mantra or a toast—and completely let go of the rest of it, only looking at the longer intention I wrote out a year, or sometimes several years, later.

When the spell feels simpler, less complex, my work is different. The big, life-altering magic I spoke of is magic that has many interlocking parts, and includes several, if not all, of what I call the Planes of Stability (which I go into in *Evolutionary Witchcraft*).

The Planes of Stability are
- Spiritual Practice
- Home and Relationships
- Physical Health
- Mental and Emotional Health
- Work and Money
- Relationship to Nature

Spells including several of these planes are too complex for us to assess what is known as "best possible outcome." There are too many moving parts. We have to let a lot more go, so allowing our conscious mind to "forget" the spell, the mantra, the meaning behind the sigil, is a useful operation.

When I do more focused magic, I like to work with the mantra and the sigil in such a way that it is kept in my consciousness. I'm still not micromanaging the outcome, but I want to be more present to many of the details of the magical operation as it unfolds. This has certainly been true of my writing and publishing magic of the past few years. I wanted to continue to work with "Words Light Worlds" and the PF Publishing flame. On one hand, I'm letting them both do their work. On the other hand, at each larger step of the way, I make sure to re-activate the magic by dressing an orange candle and working with the mantra and sigil for a month or two. After that, I acknowledge that the magic is working and set myself the task to bolster its ongoing success with more directed, daily sigil and magic work.

In a coming section, "What Does Success Look Like?", I write about the practices of daily altar work and the daily sigilization of word counts. Both help me continue to pump energy into the magic *without interfering with the larger project*, which needs breathing room and space in order for the cosmos to do its work.

As a magic worker, I have to decide what work is mine to do and what is better left to the cosmos. Both are necessary and important. If I forget one or the other, my will and intention can become tangled and confused. This shows us that the important component of answering "to forget or not forget" the particulars of our sigil or our mantra is "what is my work to do and what contributes to my doing it?"

Forgetting or setting aside the larger pattern I desire helps me exponentially because there is too much to keep track of, and I'd either drive myself crazy with trying, or rush around, over-scheduled, trying to juggle myriad balls, some of which I can't even really sense or feel. I may very well give up then, deciding the magic didn't work.

Remembering and working closely with the smaller pattern also helps me. It keeps me on track and makes it easier to show up each day to feed the magic and re-invoke my will and my intention.

"Words Light Worlds" will do what it needs to, over time. I cannot know the results over time. I can't ascertain what the consequences or effects of this spell will be. I'll make sure it's on every novel, encoded in the sigil, but that's all. Do I even recall exactly what the original spell contained? No way. And it isn't important to keep it in mind anymore.

The daily invocation of the word count sigils, and the prayers to Brigid, and the centering of my mind, heart, and soul, has to be kept in the forefront, otherwise the daily work of manifesting my will does not get done.

To forget or not to forget? We have to figure out what works for us. And until we figure that out—through the processes of trial and error and using our intuition—I recommend trying to let go of the big stuff and pay attention to the particular and proximate.

When we assess our ability to do, we can assess our magic. The more accurate our assessments, the more successful our magic becomes, and the greater our creative success.

Meanwhile, don't give up.

Invoking Liberation

Perfection is the death of art.

That is one way of looking at things. Another angle is this:

Perfection exists in the process, not the end.

All acts of creation and destruction are processes. The entire cosmos is in process. Do we look at the apple tree and think, "Oh if only it were more perfect. If only the blossoms never fell off the tree. If only the fruits were all the same exact shape and size. If only the apples didn't drop from the branches to rot upon the ground." If any of those states of "perfection" were true, the apple tree would not be an apple tree, and its process of creation would cease.

The apple tree is perfect as it is. It is perfect because it is one with its own nature, which is to cycle through the seasons, leaves falling, branches bare, leaves budding, flowers coming in, fruit ripening, fruit falling, fruit rotting on the ground to be eaten by the ants and beetles, worms and earth.

True perfection requires change. To liberate ourselves from static views of perfection isn't easy, and sometimes feels painful. To create, however, this sort of liberation is necessary, and every phase of our creative careers requires another round of liberatory practice. Sometimes this process is small and subtle, and in other phases, of course, the liberation feels more extreme.

As a writer, sometimes facing the new day's work requires one of those smaller acts of liberation. Some days, there is a sense of excitement that I get another chance to create. Other days, the part of me that wants to know what is coming doesn't want to just "Write the next sentence" as Dean Wesley Smith counsels. I want to have a better idea of the story before taking yet another risk and plunging in. So, to liberate myself, sometimes what I do is just start typing. Other times, I find the music needed to quiet the part of my brain that wants the writing to be "perfect" in the static sense of the word. The music allows me to not worry about the outcome and to enjoy the writing journey.

I once knew a poet who wrote beautifully, and gave readings in San Francisco. I loved his work. Despite having arranged his whole life to support writing poetry, this person would not submit his pieces for publication. "Why?" I asked. "Because then I cannot change them anymore," he said.

He wasn't willing to let go of his work and send it out into the world. He wanted the ability to continue crafting and perfecting it…which is another good way to kill art eventually. As creators, we can't return to last year's apples. All we can do is enjoy the fruits to come.

One key tenet of magic is also a key tenet of art and design: we must release attachment to the outcome of our process. We've gone over this before, in earlier sections, but it bears repeating. The Bhagavad Gita enjoins us to "be intent on action, not on the fruits of action." Aleister Crowley wrote of "pure will, unassuaged of purpose, delivered of lust of result."

We create in order to create. Yes, we create in order to communicate something, and we do that to the best of our abilities, but the final form cannot look like the one that first emerged in our imagination, whether that was a glimmer, a feeling, or something more fully conceptualized. If it does, we aren't allowing the cosmos to work with us.

Now, this is not to say that a master craftsperson won't come out with a finished product that looks pretty darned close to the one they sketched. But I'll bet they made several sketches from their initial idea, allowing the image to take shape, moving and changing itself according to the sweep of the hand and the way this piece wants to fit into that. It will also be somewhat dependent on mood, emotion, and the way light falls through the windows, or sound reaches the ears on that particular day. All creation, then, is co-creation.

The master knows their materials more intimately than the apprentice and therefore *does* have more control over the outcome, but they got there through many years of trial, error, experimentation, and building relationships.

Too many of us want to be at master level without having put the time and attention into the relationship with our materials and our own hearts, minds, and souls. This is a mistake. This is where some serious prayers for liberation come in.

This is as good a place as any—as we near the end of the book—to talk about beginner's luck. Beginner's luck happens because sometimes it just does. And, beginner's luck also happens because a beginner doesn't yet have preconceived notions about good or bad; they are therefore more willing to be in the flow and see what happens. Too often, though, if beginner's luck has struck, the person then tenses up and wants to repeat the process. This is too soon. Too early in the relationship. They haven't yet allowed enough of their creative process to emerge, let alone built up real skill and a sense for their art. They stumbled upon one thing that worked, or happen to be gifted enough that sheer talent won the day.

Luck and talent stall out over time if curiosity is not invoked, and the experimentation and practice that build deeper relationship aren't allowed to flourish.

We could come up with some sigils that encapsulate a breakthrough regarding liberation from perfection, too. One that works really well for me is the rune Hagalaz, which appears for me during times of needed change. The other that I work with is The Blade.

The Hailstone: Hagalaz

The ancient Nordic peoples had legends that this world was made by fire and ice. Lava runs toward ice floes, and two worlds meet. Opposition comes together, creating something new. Seeded in the hailstone, then, is one of the forces of creation. The hailstone comes with harsh fury and pelts the fields, breaking the stalks of grain and ruining the crops. However, the fields are also well watered, and new life is seeded in the fertile soil. Sometimes our carefully tended fields need to be wrecked in order for us to seed the changes necessary for new growth. Sometimes we need to look at bare ground to see where we need to begin.

The Blade

In many traditions, the blade represents the will because it stands as a physical symbol of a powerful tool shaped over time: melted down, hammered, shaped, cooled, melted... The will is consistently being worked into a form that can affect the world. But the blade is also a symbol for liberation. The blade cuts away distraction and chooses what it wants to keep. The tip of the blade points: *This* is what needs to fall away and become compost to turn into something new. We hone our will through practice. We become sharp and ready for the task at hand by the grinding away of ego, fear, and arrogance. The blade represents elegance, grace, balance, and the ability to kill what doesn't feed the work at hand. That ability is liberation itself: not to worry, but to choose.

What Does Success Look Like?

What does success look like? Is it a steady production schedule? Is it a certain number of paintings finished or words written? Is it word getting out or money coming in?

What other components dovetail with the feeling of success? Do we want to have plenty of energy? Do we want time to refill the well of inspiration? Do we want support from friends or family?

We have to keep revisiting these questions, getting more and more clear every time. If you still feel afraid or uncomfortable even asking some of these questions, it is time for another round of clearing and cleansing. And on the other end of the spectrum, if you are continuously flying off into realms of grandiosity, it is time to ground those visions into acts of will and magic you can actually do.

Earlier in the book, I distinguish between fantasy and desire. I'll state things slightly differently here: engaging with thoughts bordering on fantasy is not a bad thing. It's great to see yourself on a bestseller list, or performing to a packed house. Let your imagination run wild with those sorts of dreams! Imagine the number of people you can reach, or what you'll do if you make a pile of money and have extra to invest in your friends.

Then let it go. Let it all go.

Fantasy is not a good basis for magic. Over time, living in too-close association with grandiose fantasies only skews things toward obsession, greed, and insecurity. Magic requires us to be present with what is and what could be. We need that combination to be effective. Part of the equation is, once again, what is it possible for us to will, even not knowing what the exact outcome will look like when it comes into being?

This is difficult to write out, distant from you, with these symbols on the page trying to convey my meaning. It would be much easier if we were sitting in the same room, having a cup of tea, letting the conversation morph and shift according to what exactly it is you need to know about magic and sigils and creative success.

I'm saying that because I need to bring in yet another possible polarity, all the while knowing that most of us will shift within a full range from day to day or year to year. The polarities seem stark, but they don't have to be. I'm using them only as reminders to us all that we need to know our tendencies and look at what patterns keep us from doing the magic we need to be in the creative flow.

Some of us will go off into self-comforting fantasies that are very grand indeed. We might get trapped there, and never take the basic steps necessary to get off our butts and act toward our desires. But others of us will tell ourselves we cannot dream so big because it isn't possible for us to make those dreams come true. And so we stunt our efforts, and play too small, never reaching past our comfort levels, and never taking the risks necessary to make art that touches the hearts and minds of others, and changes us inside.

Some of us will vacillate between the two, or come up with a scenario not even written here.

So I'm going to ask us again, as I have several times already: What does creative success look and feel like to you? What do you desire?

A magic worker gets to decide what success looks or feels like, including the knowledge that it won't be the same as the initial goal or intention. We just need to comprehend that shooting for the moon requires a huge amount of preparation, time, materials, and effort. But that doesn't mean we shouldn't try.

See, that's the trouble with both grandiose fantasies and thinking too small: neither takes into account that with enough training, planning, effort, and time, we can accomplish so much. And it is my firm romantic belief that right now, the world needs us to put forth as much creativity as is possible.

I want us all to take the necessary steps to make art possible.

With all of this in mind, make another effort at envisioning or sensing what success you want.

After years of teaching around the world and having nonfiction books published, the creative success I want is to make my living writing fiction. Will I be able to accomplish this? I don't know. Do I think it is possible? Yes. Yes, I do.

And to make my living writing fiction, I need to allow myself to think big. What I cannot do is get caught up in fantasies of Oprah's Book Club, or winning the Hugo Award, or hitting the *New York Times* Best Seller lists. What I'm doing instead is studying the business of publishing on a regular basis, researching book design and covers, listening to varying opinions on what is working right now, taking writing classes to speed up my learning process…and writing every day.

Part of my magic is the mantra "Words Light Worlds" and the sigil of PF Publishing. Part of my magic is sprucing up the office altar to Brigid, Goddess of Poetry, Inspiration, Forging, and Healing, and spending time there every morning, making offerings and sitting in centering meditation.

The other thing I've done is contracted with a few friends to check in about whether or not I've met my writing goals every week. And I've been doing another, very simple, form of sigil magic. I bought a big desk calendar and wrote my daily word count goal at the top of every box, right next to the date. And every day, I write down how many words I've written underneath that, next to the project name. And every day I make or surpass my goals, I write the sigil of a checkmark in bright yellow on that box.

Why am I calling the numbers and checkmarks sigils? The numbers are a direct representation—a symbol—of my intention and I'm backing them up with my will. The checkmarks symbolize success, confirming my intention and giving the energy an extra push. When I sit down for my next writing session, the checkmark reminds me there is energy available to support my project and the fresh set of numbers reinforces the daily goal once more.

I got this "checking off the calendar" idea from indie author Joanna Penn, and it works. The numbers are magical sigils and so are the big checkmarks. They are daily, sigilized reminders of the ongoing magic of the flame and the mantra of my overall writing career.

So success to me is not just the longer-term project, but every single step in between. Every day, I have a chance to do sigil magic and reach for my success. This means I am far more likely to feel successful, which then builds the energy and gives momentum to the magic, bolstering success overall.

If I wasn't doing this, I can guarantee that the larger wish of making a living writing fiction will never come to pass. With these daily magical efforts and acts of will, however, I am successful no matter what. Even if I "fail" at the larger goal, I'm having huge successes with the proximate goals, and who knows where all this writing will take me a few years from now? I'm not micromanaging that outcome; instead I'm trusting that if I show up, the cosmos will meet me, somehow. And something will happen. I'm hoping I'll like it.

Meanwhile, I am enjoying the challenge of doing this magic, and of writing every day. I'm enjoying the heck out of the energy that mounts even on days when I'm too tired, or overbooked, or feeling uninspired, when I realize that, by careful application of my fingers to the keyboard, with my altar to my left and the daily sigils beneath my computer and keys, that the magic of wordsmithery happens, and I always get into the flow. Always. But I only get into the flow *because* of those sigils on the calendar and the "manuscript target" box that Scrivener provides that moves from red, to gold, to green as I apply my will toward the magic of my goal. If I wasn't doing this sigilized word-count magic, it would be easy for me to say, "It's feeling like too much of a slog today. I wrote a few hundred words. That's good enough. I think I'll stop now."

Since I'm doing magic, almost every day I surpass my word count goals.

Imagination, will, and the magic combined all work together, ensuring greater success.

And yes, there will come a day where perhaps I'm sick and I will actually need to rest. Because of my commitment to setting words into pixels and then releasing them into the world, I'll be able to say to myself, "Let's rest today, so we can do our magic healthy." We all have to make the call as to when we rest and when we push forward.

If we are practicing daily listening, and keeping ourselves honest with regular practice instead of haphazardly showing up, we will be able to give a more accurate assessment of what is actually necessary, rather than relying on whims, self-punishment, or letting ourselves off the hook too easily.

I'm going to ask you once again: What does success look or feel like to you?

What pathway will you choose?

Charging and Using Our Sigils

To close this book, I want to offer more ideas for how to use and charge up sigils.

My favorite method is drawing symbols on paper or carving them into candles. I've drawn sigils into sand or snow as well. I've traced them onto skin, or sliced the air with them, using a ritual blade.

My tendency is to charge up sigils with breath and sound. Sometimes I use one or the other, and sometimes I use both. Just today, when I needed more focus, I drew The Arrow, breathed across it, and set the paper on my computer to help remind me of my aim. Other times I'll begin a tone deep from my belly and let the sound resound over the rune, or I will chant the mantra associated with the symbol in order to charge it up and keep the intention clear.

Some people bring themselves to orgasm and imagine the energy shooting into the sigils, later on anointing themselves or their talismans with their juice. Still others drum to charge their sigils, or dance around the room, directing the energy raised into the sigil markings with their hands once they feel the time is right.

There are many methods worthy of experimentation. Try out several, and see which ones feel best for you.

Other ways to use sigils:

We can draw them on our arms, or over our hearts, or on our brows, using oil or lotion.

We can draw sigils in air with stick incense, allowing the glowing tip to trace the form in the air. We can then breathe in the scent of the magic, as well as letting the smoke rise up, carrying the sigil outward.

We can carve symbols into candles with a fingernail, sacred knife, a needle, or a porcupine quill.

We can make copper reliefs by wrapping thin metal around cardboard and then using a pen or a nail to emboss the shape into the metal. We can then either leave it around the cardboard, attaching a small wire to the back with glue to hang it from a wall. Or we can take the metal off the cardboard and make it into a talisman to be kept on our altars or slipped into our pockets. This sort of thin metal is easily available from art supply or craft stores.

We can use sigils as logos, symbols, and maker's marks. These can be stamped on pottery or metal, inscribed in books, or can adorn the lower corner of a canvas.

There are as many ways of making and working with sigils as there are of charging them. I've only listed some methods I've used or thought of. Let your imagination work. Develop a relationship with sigils like you do with the rest of your magic.

Then charge them up and let them do their work.

I wish you success.

A Blessing

May creativity pour through your life like quenching rain.

May inspiration bless your mind, body, heart, and soul.

May the flame of willingness burn strong within you.

May you push through toward the new light of the sun.

May you flourish, green and growing,
nurtured by fertile soil.

Make magic.
Create art.
Do your will.

The Shoot

Alphabets

Alchemical & Astrological Symbols

♈	Aries	☉	Sun
♉	Taurus	☽	Moon
♊	Gemini	☿	Mercury
♋	Cancer	♀	Venus
♌	Leo	⊕	Earth
♍	Virgo	♂	Mars
♎	Libra	♃	Jupiter
♏	Scorpio	♄	Saturn
♐	Saggitarius	♅	Uranus
♑	Capricorn	♆	Neptune
♒	Aquarius	♇	Pluto
♓	Pisces		

▵	Air
△	Fire
▽	Earth
▽	Water

The Ogham Alphabet

Letter	Sound	Name & Meaning
├	B	*Beith* — birch
╞	L	*Luis* — rowan
╞	F	*Fern* — alder
╞	S	*Sail* — willow
╞	N	*Nion* — ash
┤	H	*Uath* — hawthorn
╡	D	*Dair* — oak
╡	T	*Tinne* — holly
╡	C	*Coll* — hazel
╡	Q	*Ceirt* — apple
┼	M	*Muin* — vine
╪	G	*Gort* — ivy
╪	Ng	*Ngéadal* — reed
╪	Z	*Straif* — blackthorn
╪	R	*Ruis* — elder
┼	A	*Ailm* — white fir
╪	O	*Onn* — gorse
╪	U	*Úr* — heather
╪	E	*Eadhadh* — poplar
╪	I	*Ioadhadh* — yew
✳	Ea	*Éabhadh*
✦	Oi	*Ór* — gold
᚜	Ui	*Uilleann* — elbow
⚔	Ia	*Ifín* — pine
▦	Æ	*Eamhancholl*
ǀǀ	P	*Peith* — soft birch

Ogham is written either bottom-to-top or left-to-right along a single line, with "feathers" at the ends.

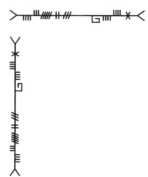

The Hebrew Alphabet

Letter		Sound	Value		Name & Meaning
א		A	1		*Alef* — Ox
ב		B, V	2		*Bet* — House
ג		G	3		*Gimel* — Camel
ד		D	4		*Dalet* — Door
ה		H	5		*Hei* — Window
ו		V	6		*Vav* — Nail, hook
ז		Z	7		*Zayin* — Sword
ח		Ch	8		*Het* — Fence
ט		Th	9		*Teth* — Serpent
י		Y, J	10		*Yod* — Hand
כ	ך	K	20	500	*Kaf* — Palm of the hand
ל		L	30		*Lamed* — Ox-goad
מ	ם	M	40	600	*Mem* — Sea
נ	ן	N	50	700	*Nun* — Fish
ס		S	60		*Samek* — Prop, support
ע		Ay	70		*Ayin* — Eye
פ	ף	P, F	80	800	*Pe* — Mouth
צ	ץ	Tz	90	900	*Tzadi* — Fish-hook
ק		Q	100		*Qof* — Back of the head
ר		R	200		*Resh* — Head
ש		Sh	300		*Shin* — Tooth
ת		T	400		*Tav* — Mark, cross

Hebrew is written right-to-left. The five letters shown with two forms have a second form used at the end of a word. For example, בנימין is the name "Benjamin".

Elder Futhark Runes

Letter	Sound	Name & Meaning
ᚠ	F	*Fehu* — cattle, wealth
ᚢ	U	*Uruz* — auroch (wild ox)
ᚦ	Th	*Thurisaz* — thorn, giant
ᚨ	A	*Ansuz* — the All Father Oðin
ᚱ	R	*Raiðo* — ride, journey, wheel
ᚲ	K	*Kenaz* — torch
ᚷ	G	*Gebo* — gift
ᚹ	W	*Wunjo* — joy
ᚺ	H	*Hagalaz* — hailstones
ᚾ	N	*Nauðiz* — need
ᛁ	I	*Isa* — ice
ᛃ	J	*Jera* — harvest, year
ᛇ	Ei	*Eihwaz* — yew tree
ᛈ	P	*Perthro* — the lot cup, chance
ᛉ	Z	*Elhaz* — elk, protection
ᛋ	S	*Sowilo* — the Sun
ᛏ	T	*Teiwaz* — the sky God Tyr, justice
ᛒ	B	*Berkano* — birch tree, beginnings
ᛖ	E	*Ehwaz* — horse & rider together
ᛗ	M	*Mannaz* — mankind
ᛚ	L	*Laguz* — water, lake
ᛜ	Ng	*Ingwaz* — the earth God Ing, fertility
ᛞ	D	*Dagaz* — day, dawn
ᛟ	O	*Othala* — home, ancestral property

Some Resources
in No Particular Order

Books, Pamphlets, and Podcasts

Oven Ready Chaos by Phil Hine
The Book of Results by Robert Sherwin
Practical Sigil Magic by Frater U.D.
Taking Up the Runes by Diana Paxson
Ogam: Weaving Word Wisdom by Erynn Rowan Laurie

The Creative Habit by Twyla Tharpe
Art and Fear by David Bayles and Ted Orland

Crafting a Daily Practice by T. Thorn Coyle
Make Magic of Your Life: Passion, Purpose, and the Power of Desire by T. Thorn Coyle

Honoring or Appropriation: Elemental Castings Episode #77 (available on iTunes or at http://www.thorn-coyle.com/videos-podcasts/podcasts/)
Demons or Angels or Something New: Everydaysigils. tumblr.com

Some Creative Blogs I Follow

Dark Matters: http://thisisdarkmatters.org/
Joanna Penn: http://thecreativepenn.com/
Dean Wesley Smith: http://deanwesleysmith.com/
Kristine Kathryn Rusch: http://kriswrites.com/
Brain Pickings: http://www.brainpickings.org/

My "Writing" list on Twitter is filled with a variety of interesting folks: https://twitter.com/ThornCoyle/lists/writing

Gratitude

I give thanks to Jonathan Korman for consultation on Hebrew and help with the tables.

I give thanks to Robert Russell for Runic consultation.

I give thanks to Raven Edgewalker for Ogham consultations. You can find her work at greenwomancrafts.com.

Jonathan, Robert, and Raven are not to blame for my interpretations!

Thanks to Dayle Dermatis for editing and formatting.

Thanks to all of my teachers, over many years time. May one thousand blessings rain upon you.

Thanks to my clients and students who continue to inspire me, and help spur me on my path.

Thanks to the Gods and Goddesses, and the cosmos, ever unfolding.

About the Author

T. Thorn Coyle is a magic worker, activist, and Pagan committed to love, liberation, and justice.

Thorn's work reaches people all over the world through spiritual direction, soul readings, vibrant workshops, and online classes. Thorn is the author of the novel *Like Water* and the short story collection *Alighting on His Shoulders: Ten Tales from Sideways Worlds*. Her spirituality books are *Make Magic of Your Life: Purpose, Passion, and the Power of Desire*, as well as *Kissing the Limitless*, *Evolutionary Witchcraft*, and *Crafting a Daily Practice*. She has also produced four music collections—two with musician Sharon Knight—and a devotional dance DVD.

Thorn believes we all have the capacity for magic.

Made in the USA
Monee, IL
27 September 2021